PEACE

FROM

THE PAST

Finding the Light

To Freedom

Through Forgiveness

A Memoir By:

Valerie "Golden" Allen

VJ Publishing House, LLC.
20451 NW 2nd Avenue Suite 112
Miami Gardens, Florida 33169
www.vjpublishinghouse.com

The author from her life and other individuals' experiences created all composites.

ISBN: 10 1939236029

"Peace From the Past"

Cover Design by: James Eagles of Miami, Florida

PUBLISHING HOUSE, LLC.

"You may not control all the events that happen to you, but you can decide not to be reduced by them."

"Maya Angelou"

Sitting Down In the Kingdom…

THIS BOOK IS DEDICATED TO THE MEMORY OF:

~CARNELL GOLDEN SR. ~

I WAS BLESSED WITH A COURAGEOUS EARTHLY FATHER, WHO DEDICATED HIS LIFE TO SERVING GOD, FAMILY, AND OTHERS…

IN TIMES OF TROUBLE, **I WAS BLESSED WITH** A STRONG SHOULDER TO LEAN ON…

BUT MOST OF ALL, **I WAS BLESSED WITH** A FRIEND

WHO **LOVED** ME UNCONDITIONALLY…

I WAS TRULY BLESSED WITH A

'DADDY'

~Letter to My Readers~

Dear Friend,

I've found peace with my past, a journey that has shaped me into who I am today. Every yesterday, last week and year has been a steppingstone, preparing me for the unknown of tomorrow. My mistakes and wrong choices, once burdens, have become my armor, equipping me to face the challenges and trials that life throws my way. My teachers have been the tribulations, dilemmas, hardships, and hard times, revealing the God-given strength within me to 'Stand!' The people who hurt me have inadvertently shown me the path to forgiveness, which has brought me peace.

My family and friends have shown me the beauty of life in the presence of good company. The lies I was told have only deepened my appreciation for the honesty I've received from others. I am who I am because of the good and bad times, the kindness and betrayal from friends and foes. But most importantly, I have discovered the transformative power of 'forgiveness,' a beacon of 'light' that has led me to freedom.

Having found my peace, I write this memoir with the hope that it will resonate with you and, perhaps, guide you toward your own path of peace and forgiveness.

Love ~ Valerie

~TABLE OF CONTENTS~

"Fight your battles on your knees, prayer is your weaponry."

~Valerie Golden Allen~

Prologue

As I looked over the selected jurors, I felt empowered and confident. I knew my fate was in their hands, but I also knew that the truth would prevail. The outcome of this case might impact the rest of my life, but I was ready to face it head-on. Life is unpredictable, but I was determined to fight for my freedom, and my son's future.

As the prosecutor brought in the states key witness, I was ready to face him. I hadn't seen Clarence since the domestic dispute ten months ago, but I was no longer afraid. I knew he was still in bondage serving Satan, and his lies wouldn't hold me back anymore. I was no longer blind, foolish, and I was ready to show the absolute truth.

As Clarence raised his right hand to tell nothing but the truth, I did not doubt that my victory was inevitable. His deceitful and manipulative ways were no match for the truth that I was about to share. Love didn't live here anymore, but justice and verity did. Returning home that evening, I decided to put my faith in God. I ordered a pepperoni pizza with wings, celery sticks, carrots, and bleu cheese for Victor, Vanessa, and I. After a warm shower, I read Psalms 91, and verse 15 captivated my spirit. I knew God would deliver and honor me. On my knees, tears welled up in my eyes, not because of fear or doubts, but because of gratitude and faith. "Even though I've made mistakes and bad decisions, God's love for me hasn't diminished. The past ten months have been a challenge, but I've overcome them. Justice will ultimately prevail, and I feel prepared to confront anything that comes my way."

"I am where I am, because of the bridges that I crossed."

~Oprah Winfrey~

~Chapter 1~

Come with me Pony, to the other side. I longed to cross the street that was always off-limits. The dazzling lights and towering buildings beckoned me. Curiosity consumed me. That day, at the edge of the pavement with my first love, I reflect back and realize, even at the tender age of three, I was daring and bold. My decision was clear: with or without Pony, I was determined to make that leap.

When the two Caucasian police officers in the patrol car spotted the two brown toddlers, barefoot, shirtless, and wearing soiled underwear while holding hands and walking alone, all I could think was, "Please, don't put me in that police car." I can't go to jail, Mama gonna tear my butt up. You see, Pony and I had walked so far that we'd become lost and couldn't find our way back home. Of course, in the 60s, things were quite different, much safer, and everybody's "Mama" was your Mama, with the permission to whip your butt too. The ageless adage, "Raising a child takes a village," has stood the test of time across generations.

The police officer stepped out of the white vehicle with red lights on top and began questioning Pony and me. My stomach started to do flips from the cereal and milk I had eaten earlier, and I had to pee so badly that my little bowlegs were shaking uncontrollably. Still holding his hand, I turned to look at Pony and noticed he had his head bowed and was crying. The officer said, "It's okay. Just tell me your names."

I hesitated for a second because I was not used to seeing police officers up close and personal. I'd only seen them on television or riding through our neighborhood. I replied, "Roe," and Pony whispered his name.

"Where do you live?" the police officer asked. Pony and I were so nervous we said, "We don't know." The officer opened the car door and told us to get in. Apprehensive, we climbed into the white car, and they took us down to the police station. Once we got to the precinct, I was the center of attention. I was introduced early to the "spotlight" as everyone bragged, "She's cute as a button." With my curly hair and muddy crossed legs, I sat on the officer's desk nibbling on melt-in-your-mouth chocolate chip cookies and sipping sweet tangy orange juice. I knew I was in trouble, but it didn't matter. I was fearless!

Pony and I had the entire community in an uproar looking for two toddlers that seemed to have vanished into thin air. Nowadays, we would have been put in state custody, and our parents would have been sent to jail for child neglect. Boy, times have changed from those "good old days," but "I" haven't. I was always into something, one way or another. I inherited the nickname "Roe" from a monstrous, terrifying bird named Rodan that debuted in its own movie in 1956. Upon further investigation, it was revealed that the bird was not an adversary but rather an ally to Godzilla, fighting for various causes. Similarly, I find myself in a similar role as a helper, facing numerous challenges throughout my journey.

I couldn't understand why she cried when Mama and the others rushed into the precinct. She picked me up and squeezed me so tight that I could barely breathe. I thought to myself, what is this? Do you mean to tell me she didn't bring her cherry tree switch? I basked in the moment because I knew

Mama had an alternate plan once she got me home. To my surprise, I didn't get a whippin' that day, and neither did Pony.

As we played marbles together a few days later, I noticed he wasn't trying to win. Pony was letting me beat him on purpose. He must have felt what I was feeling. Saying goodbye to my first love a few weeks later would be bittersweet. Although our mamas were friends and said they would keep in touch, I felt it would be my last time seeing him. My family was finally leaving Overtown and moving to Miami's up-and-coming **Liberty City**.

As Daddy and Cousin Bob finished loading the last boxes onto the truck, I skipped over to Pony and joined the other kids in a game of "Red Light, Green Light". I shouted, "Goodbye, everybody! We're leaving now!" but Pony just casually waved his hand and continued playing with the other kids. It hurt my feelings, but I knew that this was just the beginning of a new adventure for me. In the future, I would travel this road many times, but for now, Roe was off to a new adventure!

"Just don't give up

what you're trying to do.

Where there is love and inspiration,

I don't think you can go wrong."

~Ella Fitzgerald~

~Chapter 2~

What's wrong with me? This is unfamiliar territory. I can't explain what I'm feeling. This brokenness, nonchalant mannerism, and I-don't-care demeanor ... seem to dominate my daily practices. I don't cry the way I used to cry. I don't feel that sensitivity towards humanity anymore. I also don't react to others' emotions like I used to. Maybe the many pains I've endured have finally run me down. But my name is Roe. Through every trial and tribulation, over and over again, I've had to stand despite circumstances. Nothing could hold me down too long... not a man, financial crisis, or a health issue. Not even my daddy's belt could catch me; I was blessed with the gifts of fight or flight.

As I ran upstairs to grab my cell phone, I noticed the name that popped up. Darn, what does Harvey want now? He was blowing my phone up again. "Hey lady," he said. "What are you doing tomorrow evening around six? I need your support, Vanady. I'm running for city councilman."

I told him I'd check my calendar and get back to him later. I scrolled through my Blackberry to see if I was available, and to my surprise, my calendar was open. I called Harvey back a couple of hours later to let him know that I was available and would meet him and my best friend, Samantha, around six p.m. at Club MVP for the political function.

Oh well, I thought to myself. What will I wear tomorrow? Okay, nothing too sexy because I don't want to give off the wrong impression. Searching through my closet, I noticed the two-piece form-fitting baby blue pantsuit I bought from Caché a few months ago. Hold on to your man, ladies. This one here, is a showstopper.

As my best friend Samantha and I strolled into Club MVP to support Harvey in his bid for councilman, all eyes were on us. It was a quaint little group filled with businessmen/women and political figures. However, there was something in the air that I couldn't quite put my finger on. I thought, I really don't like Harvey. He's friendly, ambitious, and a go-getter, but I don't feel that something, something necessary for Roe. Honestly, I was seeing a few other men, and they all seemed to be in the same boat, full of bull crap. Although I wasn't an angel, I wasn't settling for less, again. Nodding my head in agreement, I said, "I love the new color scheme, and the room's ambiance feels good too."

As we sipped our cocktails, I saw a few familiar faces I hadn't seen in a while, so I slid off the stool to mingle with them. The pewter stilettos I'd selected to complement my suit weren't a good idea. My feet were killing me! Slowly walking back to my seat, I felt his eyes watching me.
I turned to Samantha and asked, "Who's that man? I've never seen him here before. He's staring at me like he knows me. He's sort of ugly and quirky looking. I know he isn't thinking about trying to holla at Roe."

Suddenly, in a thrilling moment, the DJ played my favorite song. The rhythm of the beat touched my soul, prompting me to leap off the stool and groove to the music with my hands, syncing my body to the lyrics and melody of "I'm Curious" by Midnight Star. While singing the words, "I'm curious about your loving. I'm curious, I want to know what's on your mind," I thought back to the curiosity of a three-year-old girl wanting to cross a forbidden street.

The next thing I knew, a quirky-looking gentleman had joined me on the dance floor without even asking. I thought he was bold; this nerd isn't trying to get with me? But being the dignified woman I am, I grooved with him to my favorite song, not wanting to hurt anyone's feelings. Surprisingly, this guy had rhythm, and a little something-something about himself. As my aching feet and I returned to my seat, he followed.

He extended his hand and said, "Hi, my name is Clarence Alexander. And you are?" I replied, "My name is Vanady. However, they call me 'Roe.'" He said, "I like Vanady better because you remind me of the Goddess Venus."

Well, one thing I can say about this guy is that he was smooth with his words and seemed very confident in himself. Although it was supposed to be our last drink, he offered Samantha and me another one, and of course, we accepted. As Clarence spoke, his conversation was strikingly interesting, stimulating, and quite pleasant, which was a big turn-on for Roe.

I thought, no way, no how! I can't explain this guy. He's not my type; he's not even in my league. He looks plain bland. Yes, I am attracted to intellects, but the physicality must also be at a certain standard. My family and friends would never let me live this down. I can already hear the questions... "Where did he come from? Do you know he's nerdy-looking and not pleasing to the eye? What does he bring to the table?" But then I reminded myself Roe is adventurous and a bit risqué.

As I gathered my purse to leave, Clarence asked, "Will I see you again?" I looked at him from head to toe, leaned over, and whispered, "Maybe."

"Spare the rod and spoil the child – that is true. But, beside the rod, keep an apple to give him when he has done well."

~ Martin Luther~

~Chapter 3~

As I reflect on my life, I realize that I was living in a place called "confusion" at that time. I loved my independence yet, longed for consistency, stability, and being the apple of one man's eye again. Truthfully, I didn't know what the hell I wanted!" You see, after surviving one of the most hellacious divorces any human being could endure, I'd made a vow to love me, myself, and I for a while. I was a female player who was only interested in having a good time, and what a man could do for me. I dated an NFL retiree, an attorney, and a club owner. It was a fun, exciting, carefree time in my life. I had no holds except my children, which I gladly embraced. But like with every piece of matter that surrounded me, I got tired of the same old game and needed a new adventure, another boundary to cross. I needed the total spotlight again! I needed to be found! But who or what could I indulge in to satisfy this intense craving?

Looking at my vision board, I was far from the goals I had set the year before. There were so many bumps, bends, and detours along the road that I needed a GPS to lead me back onto the right path. I was all over the place. I believe I must have been someone of high stature in my past life.

My Mama said that as a little girl, I would play dress up. I wanted to be like Glenda, the good witch in The Wizard of Oz. So, I would gather aluminum foil and make my crown, use a towel as my robe, put on Mama's high-heeled shoes as my slippers and grab a spoon as a wand to grant wishes. I had a heart of gold, yet I could be a little spoiled when things didn't go quite my way.

With six sisters and two brothers, I didn't have to look too far for a good time. Every Friday evening after work, we'd meet to play cards, dance, eat seafood, and get our drink on at my parents' house. My sister Lolita was always the life of the party; however, she was a troublemaker too. If the sky were blue outside, she would convince everyone that it was purple, and like fools, we would believe her. As a child, she was always in trouble. If Mama said, "Go left," she would go right. Every week, she was getting a whippin' for either being too sassy with her mouth or sneaking boys into the house when Mama and Daddy would go out. On one occasion, when she was supposed to watch over me and my two younger sisters, we heard moans coming from Mama's bedroom. We thought the television had been mistakenly left on, but to our surprise, when we pushed open the door, we watched as she tried to shove a speckled-butt boy out of our parents' bedroom window. I said, "Oooh, I'm gonna tell Mama on you!" My sisters Abigail and Liza stood behind me in amazement. Lolita started quickly convincing us we hadn't seen what we saw. She was all up in my face, and of course being Roe, I didn't back down. She grabbed me by my right arm and twisted it to make me change my mind. Of course, I resisted. As I reached back for her hair with my left arm, somehow, she got me into a chokehold. Gasping for air, I managed to bite down on her arm and free myself, and of course, the fight was on! Yes, she was older in years and more significant in size, but I was considered a little prizefighter. I swung my hands punching and scratching her face like an alley cat. She pushed me hard against the wall, making me hit my head. I got really mad. I then jumped into the air, extended my left leg, and came down with a kung-fu karate kick landing on my butt. She jumped on top of me, straddling her body over mine, and pinned my arms down. "Let me go!" I yelled. She said, "If you open your mouth one more time, I'm going to choke the life out of you!"

My two sisters were trying to pull her off me when the doorbell rang. Our cousin and her partner in crime were at the door. Barbara walked in on the mayhem with an alternative motive yelling, "Y'all need to stop!" Lolita released me, and I arose from the floor slipping in a sucker punch right to her belly. Barbara then stood between us, but I didn't care; I was ready for another round. "She choked me!" I yelled out. Abigail and Liza said, "Yes, she did, and she had a nasty boy in Mama and Daddy's bedroom. We caught him going out the window with his pants down." Barbara then asked, "Who wants to go to the candy lady's house and get some frozen cups, a hot sausage, and how about some Now & Later candies?" My sisters were suckers; they fell right into her hands screaming, "Yeah!!!" I thought, hell no! I'm not going to be bought off that easy; I'm not falling for that crap; I want blood!

When the green station wagon rolled up a few hours later, Lolita had already put on her protective gear. She now wore a long-sleeve white shirt with two pairs of slacks; she knew daddy would tear her butt up. As I told Mama and Daddy what happened, Abigail and Liza stood frozen in silence; those chumps had been bought off. Daddy yelled, "Bring me the belt," of course, like rabbits, we all scurried to locate it. When anybody got a whippin, the whole house went into silent mode. My daddy would whip you, sit down, eat dinner, and then return and finish the job. We were never physically abused, but I must say, he indeed didn't spare the rod.

Daddy was an old Southern, back-home Georgia boy with a third-grade education. In the early 1950s, he and my Mama had married, left Georgia, and headed for a better life in up-and-coming Miami, Florida. Daddy was a carpenter with gifted hands that could build just about anything. He was a great provider despite all the odds against colored men in those days. Daddy had found his niche in the construction industry. Gold Coast Construction Company, founded by daddy, would consist of men from the local community, church members, and several male family members. Daddy would work so hard until his hands would itch and bleed from the chemicals in the cement and lifting bricks all day. Every evening, upon his arrival, Mama would make sure the blue star ointment was in place to soothe his blistered hands. We would take turns rubbing and scratching his scaly, aching hands, and removing his cement-crusted smelly work boots, placing them outside on the back porch every day. This would be some one–on–one quality time with daddy as we shared thoughts.

Although he only had a third-grade education, he was very interested in ours. When report cards would come out, daddy would reward us monetarily and tell us to keep up the excellent work. Lined up, my siblings and I would present our report cards for review. Although he couldn't read, he understood the difference between an A, B, C, D, and F. His reward system consisted of ten cents for every B and twenty-five cents for every A. That was a lot of money back then, especially when you got straight A's. However, for every D or F, you were also given a few licks and placed on punishment.

My daddy did not play when it came to school; he wanted better opportunities for his children. Making the honor roll would come easy for me and three of my siblings, but for some reason, it wasn't easy for my sister Abigail. Every year, with every new teacher, she would always have the same excuse that they didn't like her. Daddy didn't have much book sense, but he had plenty of common sense and would see right through her shenanigans.

I found it so amazing how daddy could understand those construction blueprints but couldn't read or write his name. At night, if Mama didn't read the bible to him, my siblings and I would take turns for her. As an elementary school student, I decided to help my daddy. I remember bringing home some of my alphabet trace worksheets and practicing with him. I would grab daddy's hand and guide it to trace the letters along the dots. After a few months of practice and mastery, we moved to cursive. Years later, daddy could write his name instead of an X because of those worksheets and my help. He was proud of me, and I was proud of him too!

Genetics, which refers to inherited characteristics, has played a significant role in my life and the challenges I have overcome. My father was a strong, loving, and devout man who faced many difficulties and obstacles. Despite the odds against him and the limited resources, he always found a way to make something out of nothing. The lessons I learned during my childhood have proven invaluable in my adult life.

"Love makes your soul crawl out

from its hiding place."

~Zora Neale Hurston~

~Chapter 4~

I left Club MVP's exit door with Samantha; my watch reads two a.m. "OMG! I have to find Harvey and tell him I'm leaving," I said, "Go ahead Samantha, I'll meet you at the car." I turned to go back inside, but the room had gotten so crowded it was like being packed in a can of sardines. I gazed around the room again, but to no avail; I couldn't locate Harvey. So, I sent him a text message thanking him for the invite and letting him know I was leaving. As we drove home, Samantha asked, "What's up with Clarence? Did you get his phone number?" "Girl, you know he's not my type. He looks like an ugly duckling." Laughing she said, "You need to stop judging a book by its cover; he could be that knight in shining armor you've been dreaming about." I looked at her as if she had lost her ever-loving mind. Now, if anybody knew me, she did. "Don't even go there, Missy. You know my hustle, and it surely isn't the likes of a Clarence." She laughed out loud again as I pulled up to her carport to drop her home. "All jokes aside, Vanady, he seems really cool." "Whatever, Samantha. Why don't you date him?" Goodnight, crazy lady," she snickered.

The following day, as the alarm clock went off at seven-thirty, I couldn't move. I had to hit the snooze button at least twice; I was paying the price for hanging out too late on a weekday night. God, please give me five more minutes. Knowing I had to be at the office by nine a.m., I finally jumped out of bed and headed straight to the bathroom. The warm tingly shower felt so good on my weary body. Grabbing the wrinkle-free shirt and black slacks fresh from the dry cleaners, I was dressed in record time. I grabbed my blazer, briefcase, Fendi purse, and banana for the day and quickly left.

While at a red light, I was carefully applying my mascara when I heard my phone ringing in my purse. Of course, I knew Samantha was calling to talk about last night's event. She reminded me that I needed to stop being judgmental and to remember all the ballers I had dated with hidden agendas. Samantha was my girl, but this heifer was trippin'; she knew I didn't roll like that. Yes, she'd been right occasionally, but she was definitely wrong.

I parked my car in the reserved spot and said, "God, please help me make it through this day." My head was pounding, and I was weary from sleep deprivation. Sitting at my desk sipping on café con leche (Cuban coffee), the warm, sweet milk full of caffeine felt good in my mouth. It stimulated, revived, and at that time, awakened me. My secretary Greta buzzed into my office and announced that one of my annoying clients was on the phone. I was like darn, not today! It's too early in the morning; I'm not in the mood to hear another excuse from him. I needed more than what this writer was producing. I needed a story that would make my readers cringe, crave, cry, and not want to put the book down, not even when they went to the bathroom. I wanted something they could visualize and relate to, something relevant. Owning a publishing business these days took work, and the competition was fierce!

After granting the author another extension, I pondered why I'd gone into the literary field anyway. I'd been a pretty good English student, but this CEO publishing title required mental, psychological, and emotional stamina because everybody and their mama felt they had a story to tell. Choosing potential candidates was interesting. Listening to why they felt the world needed to hear their story and how it would impact other lives could be a reality show. The phrase "sell yourself" would take those hopefuls to another level. One of my clients, writing a tell-all book, shared how she made love to her man at his workplace on his lunch break in her car every day. She'd said if she didn't give it to him, he couldn't focus, would become jittery, and sometimes would suffer an anxiety attack. He needed it every morning, lunchtime, after work, and every night. He was a nymphomaniac!

Being a listening ear with a couple other staff members would highlight our afternoons. We would laugh and sometimes cry, not knowing what to expect in the following interview. As an author, I knew the horrors and hurdles that you could come up against in the publishing industry. With that in mind, I set out to change the literary world by giving authors freedom of choice, quality publications, high-end marketing, and author-partner relationships. With a desire to help struggling authors tap into the challenging industry, I believed every story is "different" and "unique," highlighting the need for a publishing company with an open mind and heart. Yes, I had a heart for people; however, it was Friday, I'd just gotten paid, and I needed to release this week's stress! The clock on the wall read four fifty-nine pm, which meant the weekend was here! Just as the clock struck five o'clock, the phone rang, and it was Samantha. Feeling the same as I was, she said, "Girl, meet me at MVP for happy hour, I need a drink." "Say no more, Chica, I'm on my way!"

I arrived at the club in no time and spotted Samantha sitting at the bar entertained by a tall, caramel-coated gentleman. I made eye contact and waved to let her know I had made it. The aroma of the free buffet was calling me, so I decided to eat something before I started drinking. I grabbed a small plate and spooned a handful of popcorn shrimp, fried chicken wings, and a scoop of spinach dip with tortillas. Despite being considered petite, I had a hearty appetite. With food in my hand, I went to the bar where Samantha introduced me to "Rodney," the caramel-coated man who wanted to hang around. I extended the courtesy by shaking his hand and saying, "Pleased to meet you." Samantha asked, "Why didn't you fix me a plate?"

I looked at her and responded, "You beat me here; if anything, you should have fixed me one." The caramel-coated gentleman said, "No worries, I'll fix you one."

After he left, I turned to Samantha and asked her, "Where did he come from, and what does he do for a living?" "I met him here just now. He says he's a chef at a hotel on Collins Avenue. All of a sudden, I felt a tap on my shoulder. I turned my head slowly to the right, looking over my shoulder, and to my surprise it was Clarence, the quirky-looking gentleman from last night's political function. He said, "I've only been here on a couple of occasions, but I couldn't stop thinking about you, so I decided to take a chance and hope you would be here." Awe, that's so sweet, Clarence. He noticed the empty bar stool beside me and asked, "Do you mind?" It's a free country, sir. Trying to display my ladylike manners, I lightly brushed my mouth with the napkin after each nibble of food. Clarence beckoned for the bartender and ordered a straight-up shot of Hennessy. "Whoa! I exclaimed. Are you sure your liver can handle that? That's the only liquor I drink and what can I get for you, pretty lady? An apple martini on the rocks, I replied. Feeling at ease, he smiled and finally rested his back against the barstool. Things were getting hyped up as people gravitated toward the dance floor, lining up for the "Cupid Shuffle" line dance. Samantha covered her Long

Island iced tea with a napkin, told me to watch it, slid off the barstool, and headed straight to the dance floor. Line dancing was one of her favorite things; she was pretty good at it. The tall, caramel-coated guy stood by and watched her from a distance. Clarence asked, "Are you going to join your friend?" No, not this time, I need to chill for a minute; it's been a hell of a week. I know how you feel, he said. "I was on edge, hoping my bid to renovate the Children's Hospital in Hollywood would be accepted."
Did you get the contract? I asked. He nodded. "That's why I was here last night. I was celebrating my success." Wow, congratulations! So, what exactly do you do for a living? He reached into his back pocket, took out his wallet, and handed me his business card. It read, "Senior Project Director" at a well-known engineering company in South Florida. I was impressed. This guy might be a potential candidate. I handed him his card, but reality slowly crept back in, reminding me that I am very visual, and he didn't quite fit the picture.

Samantha returned to her seat, quickly removed the napkin from her drink, and took a big swallow. I leaned over and whispered that I believed she had a stalker. She just laughed and started talking about her day. Samantha and I were two girls who had been through a lot together. Even our ex-husbands, with their jealous and bitter hearts, could not interfere with our friendship. We were more than best friends; we were sisters.
She reminded me that one of our friends had recently become partners in a nightclub and that tonight was the grand opening. So, we decided to surprise him by dropping by later. For now, Club MVP was in full swing, and we were enjoying the atmosphere.

Clarence sat silently, occasionally lifting his glass to sip his drink. Something was intriguing about him; he seemed refined, cultured, and quite pleasant. I was used to men trying to impress me with their wealth and status, but he was different. He was quirky looking and wore rimmed glasses. However, I found his trimmed beard sort of sexy. His calm demeanor was attractive and made me want to learn more about him.

I was known for playing hard to get and being pursued by potential male candidates, but this was a new experience. Maybe I was changing. Clarence was highly intellectual, and his extensive vocabulary turned me on. I was eager to hear more. He shared his move from Texas to South Florida. As he spoke, he used words like faith, soul, belief, and God in his scholarly phrases. It was as if he had looked into my spirit and spoke words that seemed to quench a thirst I hadn't felt for a while. I noticed that Rodney, the caramel-coated stalker, was really trying to win Samantha over. She laughed and made spicy gestures as he whispered in her ear. Knowing my friend well, I noticed the nasty girl's look in her eyes, so I kicked her to remind her of our conversation about celibacy. She and I had formed a women's group to help struggling, battered, broken, and down-on-their-luck rejected women. Our mission was to empower, inspire, motivate, educate, and help them recognize their worth. We wanted to be role models by cleaning up our disorderly lives and living up to what we spoke. We needed to make a difference in the lives of others by giving back from what we had been set free from.

Looking at my watch, I realized it was time to go. I'd been moved by Clarence's conversation, and it wasn't challenging to walk away like I usually did. This was definitely a first for Roe. Samantha did something that surprised me. She invited Rodney to accompany us to Club Ebony's grand opening. When did we start doing this type of stuff? Together, we always compromised and decided as a team. "I think he's really interesting. I might be attracted to him," she said. Wait heifer, this wasn't part of our original plan. I'm not going to Ebony's as a third party. Well, why don't you invite Clarence then? He seems like a cool guy. "When did this turn into a double date? These guys are getting in the way of our plans. You know who might be there tonight, and I want to keep everything private. She reminded me, "Vanady, you are currently single and no longer wear a wedding ring on your finger. We are both divorcees, so why should you care about what others think? Those control freaks who always want to know your whereabouts, never share theirs. It's time for you to make a statement with the nerdy guy, and maybe that will make them clean up their acts. They'll probably assume he's your brother or cousin, with their judgmental, good-for-nothing ways. Samantha had warned that going outside the norm would cause controversy, but Roe was ready to take the risk. Clarence had agreed to accompany us to the club.

As we made our way to my champagne-colored Mercedes-Benz, I asked Samantha, did she see what Clarence was driving? Not a BMW, Mercedes, or even an Escalade; he's driving a Ford Explorer! Sorry, but he just lost some brownie points.

Later, I grew impatient as we waited in the long line at Ebony's. I asked Samantha to go check who was at the front door while Clarence and Rodney chatted. Keith, a friend who co-owns the club greeted our group. He was thrilled we came to support him and led us to the front of the line. He was like a big brother to us but also a ladies' man. We got along well, playing the same games. Finding an empty table was challenging since Keith and his partner had attracted a large crowd through radio promotions, social media, flyers, and word of mouth. Drinks flowed, and everyone danced to an old-school song by Frankie Beverly & Maze.

I felt safe and secure until Jeremy with his entourage arrived. Groupies went crazy trying to get his attention. I whispered to Samantha, expressing my disdain for his behavior. We finally found a table, but before I got comfortable, I excused myself to the restroom. On my way, the radio personality spotted me and sent one of his boys to invite me over for a drink. I politely declined and went to the ladies' room. After fixing my makeup, I washed my hands and returned to find everyone sitting quietly. Clarence used his American Express Gold Card to pay for the entire table's food and drinks. Oh boy, trouble, why did he let Roe see that?

The energy in the club was just right. The DJ was spinning old school songs that had everyone vibing. But, when he played Barry White's, "You Turned My Whole World Around," Clarence asked me to dance. We moved smoothly, feeling each other's heartbeat, and I felt something I hadn't felt in a long time. Suddenly, Jeremy appeared and grabbed my hand, asking if I was avoiding him. Offering me a drink, I declined and returned to the table with Clarence. Jeremy was a ladies' man who didn't like being told no. He thought the world revolved around him and that whatever he wants, he gets.

I was walking over to greet one of my high school classmates when Jeremy grabbed me, I was ready to confront him. He asked me who Clarence was, and I told him he was a friend and that he had no right to interfere. He asked me to go to the beach for sushi, I declined, which made him mad. I used reverse psychology and told him I would return to his table later to get him off my back. I did go to his table to say hello to his do-boys, but when I returned, Clarence was gone. "Girl, I got you!" Samantha said. She handed me Clarence's business card. With a sigh of relief, I then realized that I wanted more in life and needed someone's complete attention. I needed to feel wanted and desired. I believe I was changing.

"Where there is no vision, there is no hope."

~**George Washington**~

~Chapter 5~

Awakened by the loud voices coming through my walls, I covered my head with the pillow, hoping it would silence the noise, but to no avail; they got louder. They were going at it over the TV remote control again. Vanessa wanted to watch cartoons, and my teenager Victor wanted to turn to a sports channel. They'd picked the right day to mess with me; I had a slight hangover and needed to rest my weary body from the last two nights. I yelled for them to shut up, and of course, it didn't do any good. Vanessa ran into my room with the remote behind her back, and Victor was not far behind. Mama, tell him to leave me alone, I had it first!" She's been watching cartoons for the last two hours, and now it's my turn, Mama!" yelled Victor. Removing the pillow from my head, I reached for the bottled water to wet my liquor-dry mouth because I was about to give them the business. "Listen, if I get out of this bed, it won't be pretty."

But Mama, it's not fair! Yelled Victor. "I don't give a darn right about now! Have the both of you cleaned up your rooms?" Neither responded, letting me know they hadn't done their chores. "Vanessa, put the remote on my dresser, and both of you got less than an hour to have everything spick and span, or I promise you will not go to Aunt Lolita's house for the party later!" The two walked out grumbling and headed towards their bedrooms. My sister Lolita was known for her parties. Not only was she a great hostess, but she also could throw down on some good ole soul food and they didn't want to miss that. In the meantime, I had to get over this hangover, or nobody was going anywhere.

Falling into a deep sleep, I dreamed about fish again. The old folk saying was, if you dreamed about fish, someone was pregnant. Well, one thing was for sure, it wasn't me. I'd got myself fixed after my eight-year-old baby Vanessa had been born. Lord, I wonder who it is.

In my family, kids' birthday parties always became adult parties. The music and the liquor would emerge for the adults as the sun went down on the children. Dancing was my forte, and I was good at it. My sister Judith and I were always first on the floor, trying to get things turned up. Eventually, my other sisters, Abigail, Janice, and Lolita, would join us. With drinks in hand, we would groove to songs like "You Love Me Baby" by Denise Williams and wind our hips down slow to "Flex" by Mad Cobra. You would have thought we had Caribbean roots because of how we moved!

My oldest sister, Carla, was always the party pooper. Just like when we were kids, she would remind us that Mama and Daddy would be disappointed if we didn't attend church on Sunday morning. That didn't mean anything to us; we partied until all the liquor was gone. But somehow, all of us, with bibles in hand, would make it to church for eleven am worship the way our parents raised us to do. Being raised in the church would be a valuable asset that would help me out of many situations. I was a brave, bold, feisty little something that stayed in trouble one way or the other. There wasn't much that I feared, but I did fear God. Although I would fall asleep or play tic-tac-toe with one of my siblings when the pastor was preaching, something must have stuck with me because I knew how to call on God in times of trouble.

I always knew there was something exceptional about me. I can't explain why I fought so much in my adolescence. I always felt the need to protect my siblings (and myself) from bullies or disgruntled friends. I wore a badge of honor labeled "Warrior."

My first spiritual warfare encounter came at the tender age of nineteen. I remember that amazing glow as if it was yesterday. My eyes affixed on the doorpost, I gazed at the flickering sparkles and wondered, what the hell is going on? I rubbed the sleep from my eyes, shook my head, and couldn't believe what was right before me. I was witnessing the eighth wonder of the world inside my bedroom. Amazed at the sight, I yelled to my visiting cousin, "Denise, look! Do you see what I see? Those burning candles. Where did they come from?" She said, "Girl, you are crazy. You're just dreaming; ain't no candles burning. Go back to sleep." I tried to convince her of what I was seeing. Calling me crazy again, she mumbled something, turned over, and returned to sleep.

As a young and inexperienced person, I was not aware that I was having my first spiritual encounter. God conveyed a message through those candles, indicating that He wanted my attention and devotion. My grandmother used to say that "God looks after babies and fools," He protected me even though I acted recklessly and without thinking. The vision I saw did not slow down my wild and adventurous self. I was often, too much for my own good.

"Whatever we believe about ourselves
and our ability comes true for us."

~Susan L. Taylor~

~Chapter 6~

As I switched out the black Fendi purse for the brown and beige Gucci that would complement my Jimmy Choo brown pumps, I noticed the business card lying at the bottom. He hadn't crossed my mind until yesterday when the preacher talked about how God was closing doors and opening new ones—including people. It was early Monday morning, and although I had a ton of paperwork on my desk to complete, I would call Mr. Alexander later. When Greta buzzed into my office to tell me the annoying client was here to see me with a manuscript, I told her, Okay, send him in. Good morning, Ms. Vanady, he said. What do you have for me, Mr. Gillard? Well, I had to lock myself in this weekend and read what I wrote from beginning to end and see how to take it to the next level as you recommended. Hand it to me Gil, I will be in touch."

My, how time flies by; when I looked up, it was already four-thirty, and I hadn't even called Clarence yet. I reached into my purse to retrieve his card to say hello. The phone rang three times and then went to voicemail. I hesitated to leave a message, especially on the first try, but I did. My phone rang on the drive home from work, and I rummaged in my purse to find it. Damn! I'd missed the call because of my make-up bag, unopened mail, credit cards that had fallen out of my wallet, scattered dollar bills, and everything else but the kitchen sink piled on top of each other. Vanady, this is ridiculous, I thought. This purse costs too much for you to treat it like a garbage dump. You got to do better, Girl.

The cell phone screen read a missed call, and it was Clarence's number. Okay Vanady, remember; you got to play the game right. You are a wiz at this. Don't get too anxious. You have to make him sweat. So many thoughts were running through my mind like never before. God, what is going on with me? Am I falling for someone I don't quite know except for a few hours of conversation over a few nights? Who in the hell is this man? Gathering my composure, I hit the redial key on my cell phone. I don't believe this crap! His phone went to voicemail again. We were playing phone tag, or maybe Clarence was a gamer—like me. Oh well, I am not leaving another message, I thought, so I abruptly hung up the phone.

Waiting in the drive-thru at Pollo Tropical to grab dinner for the kids, my phone rang again. However, it was resting right before me on the dashboard this time. "Hello," I answered. The deep voice on the other end of the line said, good afternoon, Venus., "Excuse me sir, but I believe you have the wrong person." He laughed and said, Ms. Vanady, you are indeed a unique lady. That I am, Mr. Alexander, and then some, I affirmed. He began the conversation by asking me about my day, and I, in turn, asked him the same.

When I reach the drive-thru window, we were laughing as if we had known each other for a while. Switching over to **Bluetooth** to speak while driving home, I discovered Clarence, and I had some things in common. Like me, he enjoyed watching old movies, reading, watching the Miami Heat basketball team, and listening to jazz music. This guy was turning out to be quite interesting. As I hit the button on the electronic remote to raise the garage door, my son Victor ran to the car to grab our weekly Monday dinner. He's a growing teenage garbage disposal. However, his timing was perfect because I held my cell phone to my ear with one hand while the other held my briefcase, with my purse slung over my shoulder. Clarence and I talked for at least two hours that evening, which was mind-blowing. He asked if he could call me tomorrow, and of course, I said yes. This guy had me thinking and wondering about things I hadn't thought of in quite a while. Okay, Vanady, stop it girl! That curious trait has gotten you in lots of trouble throughout your life. Now, calm down and let nature take its course my inner being whispered.

Settling in for a night of sweet sleep, I was startled by my phone ringing. The voice on the other end said, "Mama, I'm pregnant." Recognizing it was Vivica, I asked my daughter what she was saying. "Mama, I'm so sorry, but I'm going to have a baby." Dropping the phone, I was despondent. It was as if time stood still, and I couldn't feel, hear, or speak. I couldn't do a darn thing but look at the ceiling. Pissed off, I yelled, "girl, I sent you and Vertisa off to college to educate yourselves, not to get pregnant by some piss-tailed boy."

But Mama, I graduated with my bachelor's degree and am halfway through the master's program. I promise I don't know how it happened. Well, I can tell you how it happened; instead of focusing on your studies, you were partying with that sorority and issuing out your 'peach' all over the place! Mama, I have only been with one guy for two years, and we always used protection. I can't explain it," "You don't have to explain it, your butt is knocked up! So, what are you going to do?" He wants to marry me, Mama! Marry you? You sound excited! How in the hell is he going to take care of you and a baby? Is he in school? Does he have a job? Where is he from? Who is his family? Mama, I feel so sick, I need to lie down. I can't even look at food without throwing up. Please forgive me; I'm still going to make you proud. It suddenly dawned on me who the fish in my dream was. Oh my God, my daughter was the fish! This is crazy! Have you been to the doctor yet? Yes, ma'am. How far are you, Vivica? I'm about eleven weeks. Listen, as soon as possible, you must call your daddy and tell him what's happening with you because it isn't coming from me. Okay, Mama, I will do it tomorrow. All right. Call me when you finish talking with your dad, Good night.

"Take the first step in faith. You don't have to see the whole staircase, just take the first step."

~Dr. Martin Luther King Jr.~

~Chapter 7~

Over the next few weeks, we continued to see each other. Clarence was the perfect gentleman, taking me out to dinner and the movies but always respecting my boundaries regarding physical intimacy. When he invited me to his home for dinner, I accepted but insisted on bringing dessert. The grilled steak he cooked was moist and perfectly seasoned, and the baked potato and steamed broccoli complemented it perfectly. We talked for hours, sharing stories about our past relationships, children, and five-year plans.

As the night drew to a close, he asked me to share a slice of cheesecake I had brought, and I agreed. The dessert was delicious, and we savored it with a glass of wine as we continued our conversation. However, I had to remind him I had work the next day and couldn't stay too late. Clarence was understanding, and we said our goodbyes with a promise to talk and see each other again soon. The next day, he called me, and we talked for over three hours. Clarence asked me out to dinner again, and although I agreed, I made it clear that I would drive my own car. He sent me flowers at my office, and while it was a sweet gesture, I decided to run a background check on him before I went further with Mr. Alexander.

At the restaurant, I took charge and chose the wine for us. We had a pleasant evening, but I made sure to keep things moving at a pace I was comfortable with.

"A life spent making mistakes is not only more
honorable,

but more useful than a life spent doing nothing."

~George Bernard Shaw~

~Chapter 8~

My daughters were coming home for Mother's Day, and their first priority was to meet my sweetheart, Mr. Alexander. Clarence and I were deeply in love, spending every possible moment together, craving each other like a drug. Vivica, who was pregnant and had swollen feet, could barely keep up.

As we rushed to meet Clarence for lunch, my daughters started asking questions about him. Vertisa asked, "What's he like?" Vivica replied, "Well, he's nice but talks properly." "No, he's what we call intellectual,'" I countered. "Although he's from the West Coast, he attended a predominantly white university and picked up on their pronunciation."

Vivica didn't mind, saying, "It doesn't matter to me. He's your man, and I hear he gives you nice things." Vertisa wanted to get the meeting over so we could rest before our night on South Beach. I was exhausted from the long drive the day before and needed to nap before our evening plans.

After parking, the girls left the car feeling hungry, curious, and ready to spend Clarence's money. "Okay, ladies, let's be nice and polite." With a sly grin, Vivica replied, "Mom, you're overthinking. You know you raised us well, right? We're nice and non-judgmental girls." "Yes, Mom. I hope he doesn't look like Mr. Peabody, the professor, like Vanessa thinks," Vertisa added with a chuckle. "Stop it now! If either of you try me today, I promise you'll regret it." "Okay, we're just joking," Vivica said. Sitting in the booth with the cushioned backrest felt much better than the wooden table and chairs we were first seated at. Clarence did his best to be friendly and attentive, asking Vivica how she was feeling and when the baby was due. He was so generous, telling them to order whatever they wanted, which pleased them. With their expensive taste, those girls ordered appetizers and Maine lobsters as their lunch entrées. I felt like they were up to something. Clarence invited the girls to his home to grill before they went back to school. He seemed to be trying too hard to win them over.

Under the table, I grabbed Clarence's hand and whispered to him to relax, telling him, "They won't bite." He smiled and squeezed my hand. The girls thanked him for the delicious lunch and told Clarence he was "really cool." He walked us to my car, opened our doors, and wished us a safe drive. I kissed him as I drove off, and Vivica said, "Mom, he seems nice, but I don't mean to burst your bubble. He was trying too hard for me." Vertisa added, "I agree, and I can't quite put my finger on it, but I sense something off about him." "I value your opinions, but this guy is different. He treats me like no man ever has. Clarence would jump in front of a moving car for me, promising me the world. I believe he's the one."

"Mama, I have never heard you talk about any guy like this. What has he done to you?" Vivica asked. "He treats me like I matter, as if I am the most important thing in his life. He recognizes the queen in me by not putting me on a pedestal because he knows I was born to be on a throne. He respects and honors my worth and allows me to walk in it. He may not be the most handsome man, but he is the best, and that's good enough for me," I boasted. "Whoa," said Vivica. "Mama, it's your life, and you are a grown woman. If you're happy, we're happy; however, we had to say what was on our minds and hearts." "Well, I hear and respect what you girls are saying, but it's too late." "What do you mean it's too late?" Vivica asked.

The bell saved me as my phone started ringing. It was my sister Lolita. "Roe, what's up?" she yelled. "Where the hell have you been? You missed the last two Fridays at Mama's house and didn't even show up for Nicky's baby shower on Saturday. Who is this guy that I'm hearing so much about? I have to meet the man who has managed to slow your fast butt down."

"Lolita, you are tripping; you know my name and everything it stands for." "Well, he must have some serious paper and know how to lay the pipe down if I know my little sister." "Missy, I was going to invite him for Father's Day dinner at Mama's house next Sunday." "What! You're bringing somebody to Mama's house! Oh, hell no! I ain't waiting that long. You two come by my house on Saturday, and I will cook something for both of you. What does he drink?" "Girl, he's strictly a Hennessey man, and you know I love my wine." "My bar is almost empty from hosting two NBA Finals parties. I need to restock." "What time do you want us to come by Lolia?" "Around six pm would be fine." "Okay, let me talk to Clarence to ensure he has nothing planned."

My sister Lolita has had her share of ups and downs. Two years ago, my niece, her oldest daughter, Teresa, had finally, been approved after being cleared by all her doctors to have gastric bypass surgery. You see, Teresa was morbidly obese and had suffered a heart condition from birth. The week before she was scheduled to undergo surgery, she went on a food binge, literally eating an entire eight-slice pizza all by herself. She ate anything and everything in sight. She thought, "I'm going to lose the weight anyway, so let me enjoy whatever I want now."

The following day, after the whole pizza binge, Teresa became so ill that Lolita had to rush her to the nearby hospital. After a few nights in the hospital and a severe doctor warning, Teresa was permitted to go home the following day.

Lolita had a conversation with Teresa the night before she was supposed to leave the hospital. She was very excited to go home to her one-year-old daughter and spoke about preparing for her life-changing surgery. Her dream was to lose two hundred pounds, buy a leather jacket with shorts, and ride a motorcycle through the streets of Miami.

Unfortunately, something happened in the early morning while she was going to the bathroom. Hours later, my niece was found dead on the hospital floor due to a massive heart attack. The news of Teresa's death shook our closely-knit family to the core. It was such a traumatic event that we had to call paramedics because Lolita was screaming, experiencing shortness of breath, and losing control of herself.

To make matters worse, my cousin Bernice was so overwhelmed with grief that she suffered a heart attack in the middle of Lolita's living room, falling face down and becoming unresponsive. Just before the ambulance arrived at Lolita's house, amid our grief, we gathered around Bernice's lifeless body and prayed fervently.

On that day, by God's mercy, Bernice started breathing again, and when the paramedics finally arrived, they took Bernice instead of Lolita. She was quickly placed on a breathing machine. However, two months later, Lolita's only son, Langston, who had gone to college in Tallahassee, got into trouble at a party with his friends and was sent to prison. Due to a new gun law in Florida called "ten-twenty-life," implemented just a year earlier, Langston was faced with a mandatory twenty-year prison sentence, and our family had to spend over $30,000 in legal fees.

After much prayer, debate, and negotiating, he accepted the ten-year prison sentence plea bargain. But there was more to the story. Tiona, Teresa's only child whom Lolita had helped raise since she was born, would be taken away by her insensitive, absent father. This news pushed my sister into a deep depression, and she was slowly dying from a broken heart. She had given up on life. And then, a miracle happened. God heard the prayers of the righteous. One day, Lolita heard a voice in her isolated, darkened bedroom that said, "Go to the hospital, now!" And she did. The doctors diagnosed her with pneumonia, a blood clot in her lung and right hip, and heart failure. She was in bad shape physically, mentally, emotionally, and spiritually.

I remember how every time we talked, she would ask repeatedly, "Why me, Roe? Why has everything I love been taken away? What did I do to deserve all this pain? My daughter is gone, my son is locked away for ten years, and now the baby that I helped nurture from birth is gone. Why me?" All I knew to say was what I had heard the elders say… "Lolita, I don't have all the answers, but God will reveal His plan for your life in the sweet by and by."

"I shared the story of Jesus' crucifixion with her and emphasized that God was still in control no matter how things appeared. I advised her to not rely on her understanding or others, but to trust God, and be assured that His plan was to bless her and not harm her. He had not abandoned her; only He could lead her through this difficult time. I reminded her that she did not have a plan B and must return to her first love, plan A, which was God." I told my sister that her surviving eight-year-old daughter Dominique needed her. Despite going through numerous difficult experiences, Lolita managed to keep her sanity and escape every problematic situation. She has been a strong and resilient person, still standing.

"Defining myself, as opposed to being defined by others, is one of the most difficult challenges I face."

~Carol Moseley-Braun~

~Chapter 9~

Arriving at Clarence's home around 8:00 pm had become routine for me, at least four days a week for the past three months, unless he was away on business. As I reached for my purse, I noticed a lady in a white Mercedes-Benz slowly driving by, looking at me with a smirk. I wondered who she was. Before I could knock on the door, Clarence had already opened it. He picked me up, kissed me passionately, and said he missed me. In my sassy tone, I asked, "Dude, I just saw you last night. What's up with all this love?" "I'm glad you asked, Vanady, because I can't do it anymore." "Do what, Clarence?" "I cannot go another night without you in my arms. I want to come home every day to you and the kids. Like food and water, babe, I need you to survive."

"So, what are you saying?" He replied, "Well, my place can hold us for a little while, but I want you to go out and find a nice big house to accommodate all of us as soon as possible. I want a family." "Hey, slow down, guy! I mean, where is all this coming from?" "It's coming from here, inside my heart, soul, and very being. It's coming from me. Please, babe, I'm so in love with you," he pleaded. "Wow! Please let me pray about this, Clarence." He seemed confused and asked, "Pray?" "Yes, that's what I said, pray. Do you have a problem with that?" "No, not really, Vanady. I know you go to church sometimes, but I didn't know it was all that." "Yes, it's all that and then some. I love God and talk to Him daily, whether you know it or not." "Well, good for you, Vanady. That's great news."

"Hey Clarence, I wanted to tell you about something that happened earlier. When I parked my car, a lady drove by in a white Mercedes and gave me a nasty look as if I had done something wrong. Do you happen to know her?" Clarence replied, "I don't know anyone in South Florida who drives a white Mercedes. She was probably lost or mistook you for someone else." I replied, "It's strange, but I'm not too worried. I can take care of myself. By the way, why was your phone off the hook?" "I was just hanging up with my dad when I heard your cars engine. I couldn't resist greeting you with open arms." Awe, you're always so sweet, Clarence. My sister Lolita invited us to her house on Saturday at around six p.m. Can you make it?" "I have to check on a site in downtown Brickell at ten a.m., but other than that, my day is open. Let her know we'll be there. Now, is she the crazy one you were telling me about, the one who is always in the middle of everything?" he asked. "First, I can call my sister crazy, but hell if you can. She likes much attention," I said. "Mmmm…. sort of sounds like you!" he smirked. I rolled my eyes and said, "Oh, I know you didn't go there, 'Mr. Clingy'! Vanady, are you coming over? Vanady, please don't leave. Vanady, when are you coming back? Oh where, oh where is my little lost Vanady?" I mocked.

In a cavalier, debonair, pompous voice, he replied, "Damn right. You're my sheep; this shepherd is calling his babe home, and I mean home for good! Come over here and show me how much you love me!"

A month later, as I waited for the moving truck, which was thirty minutes late, my anxiety was kicking in. I couldn't explain this feeling within me. I couldn't shake it off. Clarence had needed to leave on company business out of town but had planned everything for a smooth transition for the kids and me. Finally arriving, the driver explained there was a significant traffic jam on I-95 due to a fatal car accident. As they carefully loaded the truck with my furniture and fixtures to be placed in storage, I felt a sense of gloom. An independent woman, I had been making it on my own, and now I was giving up that independence. I wondered if I was making the right decision. I had prayed about it and listed the pros and cons of living with a man in my journal. However, I had some mixed feelings. Clarence Alexander was loving, hard-working, attentive, compassionate, and a generous man, but was it enough? "GOD, please send me a sign?" I pleaded, but nothing happened.

Finally settling into Clarence's lovely, contemporary home, I knew I had to adjust his bachelor pad. The Rooms to Go furniture was in synch with its lovely fixtures and accessories; however, that picture with the shirtless man bound in chains with his head bowed in his hands was too depressing for me. I had asked Clarence why he'd chosen such strange artwork. He responded that the man in the picture was him during a challenging period of his life, so he kept it there to remind him of where God had brought him from. Hearing him mention God in his response was good enough for me, but that picture would be relocated to the hallway near the bedroom.

I gave Vanessa and Victor an assignment to go through our boxes and place everything that didn't belong inside the house in organized stacks on the shelves in the garage. Known for being a little OCD, I used Lysol and Pine-Sol to clean everything from the ceiling fans down to the toilets and crevices of the tiled floors.

My biggest project was the main bedroom. It had been patiently awaiting me; it needed a woman's touch. Stripping the bed of its linens, I pushed off the queen-sized mattress and lifted the box spring to vacuum underneath it. I noticed something black stuck in the bottom of the box spring. As I moved in to get a clearer view, I recognized a small black pillow tucked inside one of the slats. I asked myself, "What the hell is this?" Then I heard a whisper saying, "Don't touch it." Oh God, what am I supposed to do? This is creepy."

I dashed to the kitchen drawer and grabbed the barbecue grill tongs to pick the pillow up. The black pillow was covered with round white mildew spots. OMG! Again, I heard that voice, and it said, get rid of it immediately! Oblivious to anything else going on, I quickly obeyed the voice, ran to the dumpster, and dropped the pillow in. When Clarence called that evening, I shared with him what I'd discovered, and he was in awe. "Babe, I will be home tomorrow night, and we will get to the bottom of this." After hanging up with Clarence, I called my sister Lolita to discuss what I had found under the bed. In her loud voice, she said, "Girl, that sounds like witchcraft to me! What did you do with the pillow?" "I threw it into the dumpster," I told her.

"I can't believe it! You were supposed to burn it! You have no idea who that guy was involved with before you. You need to talk to him and find out everything about her, where she came from, and if he's up to something. Come to think of it, where is he from? I don't trust these guys at all," she said urgently. "By the way, how did you learn about witchcraft, Lolita?" "Do you remember Lucius, the guy from the Caribbean I used to hang out with? He told me about Voodoo, Santeria, and Roots. That stuff is real, and it can mess people up." "Stop saying that, Lolita. It's not real. I was always told that it won't harm you if you don't believe in it." "You sound like a naive fool," she replied. "It's in the Bible about witchcraft and principalities. You better get with it, Roe."

After our conversation, I felt uneasy, so I poured myself a glass of wine to calm my nerves. Then, I knelt and prayed: "Father God, forgive me if I have stepped outside your will. Please show me the way. Your word says you will be a light upon my feet. I am weak, and I need your direction and protection. Something is not right, and I need you to expose anything that is not from you. My grandmama always said you care for babies and fools. I may be foolish and blindly in love, but please care for me. Amen."

I couldn't sleep that night and had strange dreams. The next day, I had a headache from the wine and a lack of sleep. I took a Tylenol PM to help me sleep. Clarence and I had often slept in that bed, but that night was different. He had better have answers to what was going on. Something wasn't right.

"I have learned over the years

that when one's mind is made up, this diminishes fear."

~Rosa Parks~

~Chapter 10~

I was waiting at the guard gate for the realtor to show me a lakefront property. I felt exhausted from the night before and couldn't stop thinking about everything that had happened. My sister Lolita had talked about something that worried me, and I couldn't help but wonder who the woman Clarence had been involved with before me was. I also needed help understanding the witchcraft stuff she mentioned. I wanted this day to go by quickly so I could talk to Clarence about the situation. Suddenly, Mrs. Reynolds, the realtor, pulled up beside me and asked me to follow her. As we drove through the upscale community, I couldn't help but imagine my kids playing outside on the beautifully landscaped lawns. My, my, my, this is nice, I thought. As we drove up the driveway, I didn't have to look any further; this was home. Mrs. Reynolds agreed to meet again in two days to show Clarence the property.

When he came home that evening, I fell into his arms and held him tight. Grabbing me by the chin, he lifted my mouth to his and laid the most delicious kiss on me. My man was one of a kind. I was so blessed to have someone love me the way he did. However, we needed to discuss what I had found stuffed under his bed. Waiting for the right opportunity, I poured the both of us a glass of wine and lowered the volume on the television. He talked about his trip and the deals he'd been able to seal. He then opened the door to talk about the pillow, and of course, I walked in, asking, "Clarence, why was a black pillow stuffed under your side of the bed in the box spring?"

"Babe, I promise I have no idea what you're talking about." "Okay, Clarence, come on now, somebody had to put it there. They stuffed it into the box spring and sprinkled some liquid on it. Whatever they used, it mildewed over time. You could see the sprinkled round white spots all over it. Who were you involved with before me? I can't help but feel there's something you're not telling me." "Vanady, I was seeing this lady named Gillian for about nine months," he replied. "Did she have access to your house, Clarence?"

"I gave her the key when I went on a business trip because I was having some furniture delivered." "Where is she from?" "I believe she's from one of those small Caribbean islands; I'm not sure, baby," he said. "Somebody is up to something because I have never felt like I did last night in your bedroom. It was like something out of a scary movie; it was eerie. How long before you met me did you see her?" "Honestly, Vanady, I believe the woman has some serious issues." "What kind of issues, Clarence?" "Well, she would show up at my job unexpectedly. She would ride by my house when I didn't answer her phone calls, almost like a stalker, babe. She's still been calling my job and appeared on my doorstep a few weeks ago. I was going to tell you, but I felt it wasn't important because I told her I was in a relationship and to never come to my house again." "Did she stop calling you?" "No, Vanady. I'm telling you; the lady got some problems." "Why did you break up with her?" "Babe, she was like that woman in the movie Fatal Attraction. This woman would do some of the weirdest things, like cook every day for me and expect me to come to her house and eat. I started getting these stomach aches, and crazy things started happening when I was around her, and when I was away from her, something would always make me feel like she was near. It was wild and creepy. I can't explain it, Vanady." "Is there anything else about this Gillian person I need to know?" "No, babe. That's been over for a while, and

I made my choice." Changing the subject, he said, "Now tell me how the house hunting is going." I told him I'd found the cutest four-bedroom, two-story mini-mansion in the township, west of I-75, in Broward County. The architecture was unique. It had a big backyard with plenty of fruit trees and a beautiful lake nearby. "How much is it going to cost me, Vanady?" "It's within the budget you gave me. The realtor will show it to us on Tuesday evening when you get off work." With a look of approval, he said, "Okay, I'm ready to leave this place and for us to move to the next level." "The next level? What are you talking about, Clarence?" "Vanady, I watch how you pray at night and always thank God for everything. I want to make an honest woman out of you; I want you to be my wife." Taken aback by Clarence's statement, I, in turn, suggested, "Let's get the house first."

"Nobody's as powerful as we make them out to be."

~Alice Walker~

~Chapter 11~

My sister Lolita had pulled out all the punches and thrown down on some serious seafood. The fried fish, shrimp, conch fritters, and steamed crabs hit our nostrils as we entered the door. Introducing Clarence to Lolita and her boyfriend Charlie was an event within itself.

Lolita was a straight-up fool! She told Clarence to turn around so she could take a good look at him, and then she said, "Man, you must know how to lay it down because my sister ain't no joke. She's spoiled and gets whomever and whatever she wants." She grabbed him by the arm, led him to the bar, and announced, "Anything I say, please don't take it personally because Lolita isn't feeling any pain right about now." She added, "I started getting my drink on early, and everybody else needs to catch up." Lolita was torn up from the floor up. I'm so glad I had given Clarence a brief description of her; because anyone else would have thought she was a certified lunatic.

After devouring the seafood, Lolita started to get a little nosey questioning Clarence about where he was from and what had brought him to South Florida. She then disclosed what I had told her about the pillow. I wanted to strangle her. "I will mess up anybody that tries to harm my sister or any member of the family!" To change the flow of things, Charlie, her boyfriend, rose from his seat and asked her to dance to Betty Wright's most famous song, "Tonight, is the Night," one of Lolita's all-time favorites. Clarence and I joined in on the dance floor, and the atmosphere quickly changed. Despite Lolita's short emotional exposé, it resulted in a great evening.

Riding back home, I noticed Clarence was a bit quiet. I asked him, "Is there anything we need to discuss, babe?" He looked at me and said absolutely nothing. Wow! I thought to myself, this is a first. When we reached home, Clarence quickly headed to the shower leaving me alone in the living room. My mind was running overtime. Blaming myself, I said to God, maybe my past hurts have got me feeling this way. Father, I can't put my finger on it, but something is not right. Clarence came out of the shower, put on his pajamas (a first), and went straight to bed. Darn, was it that serious? I guessed, being a woman who had been loved, unloved, rejected, neglected, hurt, abused, misled, heartbroken, down and out, lied to, accused of, and fooled by the foolish, I was a bit vulnerable and weak. I needed to be loved. I needed to be wanted. I needed to breathe. I didn't have the strength to stand alone then; I was weak and unthinkingly ignored all the red flags, including something within that was speaking volumes. God, I need thee... Please save me from me.

A couple of days later, Mrs. Reynolds, the realtor, met Clarence and me on that rainy Tuesday evening. Clarence loved the house. He immediately took out his checkbook, and we both signed the contract. The house was ours. Later, while wrapping glassware for the move, I told Clarence, "My God, this moving thing is getting the best of me." Though Clarence had hired a moving company; there were several small things that only I could take care of it, which must be done with tender, loving care. The new house was immaculate. Our main bedroom was a suite within itself. The house's first floor was marbled with the most tasteful crown molding to enhance the beautiful colored walls that seemed to want to jump out at you. The stainless-steel appliances took my kitchen to the next level. I also wanted new furniture; everything was fine with what we had, but I wanted a new start, a new beginning. While at the furniture store, Clarence told me to choose whatever I wanted, and being "Venus," as he called me, I wanted beauty and quality. I was so overcome with joy and the new house with the new furniture that I wasn't paying too much attention to his moodiness. As I fixed his plate for dinner and passed it to him, he grabbed me by the wrist and said, "Babe, I need you to do something for me." "What is it, guy?" "Vanady, please keep me in the church because sometimes these voices in my head tell me to do wrong things that I don't want to do. I can be a nasty mother-****!" Shocked at what he'd just said, I asked, "What are you talking about?" "I can't explain it babe, but sometimes I hear these voices telling me to say and do evil things. I have to tell you because I love you and I believe that with your help, I can overcome this thing. I have never told anyone about this other than you. That's how I know I love you, which makes you the key. Please pray for me," he pleaded. I was stunned at what I had just heard. "Stop playing games Clarence, you're a sweetheart. You are one of the kindest people I have ever associated myself with. Don't speak that stuff into existence. The devil is a liar!" "Well babe, don't ever say I didn't tell you."

As the weeks passed, I noticed little behaviors and uncanny ways about Clarence I had never detected before. I said, "Okay, Vanady, maybe you're being too hard on him because you have had a couple of relationships that didn't turn out quite how you wanted them to. You need to face and change the woman in the mirror." But as I did a self-analysis, I couldn't quite come up with anything except that I loved to shop, kept an immaculate clean house, and was a great cook.

Although I was initially skeptical, Clarence's confession left me feeling uneasy. I started paying closer attention to his behavior, hoping to find some explanation for what he had said. However, the more I observed, the more convinced I became that something serious was wrong.

I cooked his favorite homemade dishes, communicated with him daily, and expressed my love and appreciation for everything he had done for my children and me. I even made love to him like he was my King, but then I realized that God is the true King, and He should always be the center of my joy. I was turning out to be just like him, isolating myself from everything and making myself available at his every beck and call. I couldn't believe what was happening to me. I will never forget the night Clarence asked me to be his wife again. I wasn't easily led to say yes, which infuriated him. As a director responsible for so many, he was used to people jumping through hoops at his command and having things done his way or not at all. Although I posed a challenge he couldn't control, Clarence's mood swings left me speechless as the weeks passed. When he came home from work, he asked, "Have you decided yet, Vanady?" If I responded, "I'm still praying about it and needed more time," he would give me the silent treatment. His behavior hurt me deeply, and I felt like I was being bullied into marrying him. Despite this, I was unsure if this was the sign I had been praying for, I felt weak.

Clarence began to display characteristics of a person with deep emotional and psychological issues. He repeatedly emailed me at work, asking, "Are you going to marry me?" or "I thought you said you loved me." These actions left me feeling confused and in despair.

After a month of this atrocious roller-coaster ride, I finally gave in. On a cloudy Friday afternoon, May 10th, to be exact, I became Mrs. Clarence Alexander in front of my eight-year-old daughter and a justice of the peace. Despite my gut screaming no, I raised my hand and said, "I do."

"Not everything that is faced can be changed,

but nothing can be changed until it is faced."

~James Baldwin~

~Chapter 12~

A few weeks after our nuptials, I addressed my new husband about his family on the West Coast in California. "When can I meet your family?" "You don't need to meet those crazy folks, babe." "What could be so bad that would make you say something so mean about your family?" "Well, my mama is psychotic. After forty years, my daddy thinks he's still at war in the Marines. My siblings are struggling with their demons. Must I go on, Vanady?" "Hey, slow down, dude. Where is all this coming from? You never said such vicious things about your family before." "Well, it's time to be real about them and their issues. My grandma, who died a few years ago, was the only one who truly loved me." "Come on guy, you sound like some spoiled brat harboring grudges from the past. It's time to forgive and forget. I don't care what problems they have going on, they are still your family, and I want to meet them." He then mumbled something under his breath and turned the volume up on the television. How rude! "I'm not playing with you, Clarence! It's time to let go and let God." I had no idea what I had opened up. I had awakened a giant. I had raised the dead. "I want your mother's phone number, Clarence." "Vanady, please just let it be." "No, I want to know my in-laws. Now give me your mom's phone number." "Okay, I will give it to you tomorrow." "I'm not playing, I want to know your family just like you know mine." "Vanady, please pour me a shot of Hennessey, babe." "Honey, they can't be that bad. Just look at you; somebody did something right." He laughed and, smirking, said, "If you only knew." "Well, I don't know, and that's why I'm trying to connect."

Two days later, Clarence handed me Ms. Dina Alexander's phone number in California after work. I decided to wait until about nine pm to call her since we were in the Eastern Time Zone, which meant she was three hours behind us. The soft-spoken woman on the phone was surprised to hear my voice and to know her baby boy was married and doing fine. We talked for over an hour about her health, Clarence's siblings, her grandchildren, the weather, my children, my occupation, etc., and I ended with, "We're coming to California real soon." She was ecstatic! "Okay, great, Vanady! My home is your home; I can't wait to meet my daughter-in-law and finally see my son!" I handed Clarence the phone, but he hesitated to take it. What could be so bad that her biological son would talk negatively about this sweet-sounding lady? I needed to get to the West Coast and get there fast for my sake and his.

We arrived in California a month later, and waiting at the baggage claim was a pain. With Clarence's silent demeanor on the airplane, everything started wrong. The airline had lost my luggage and could not locate it on any other flight. In addition, Clarence started to act a little finicky and impatient as we waited for the airline employees to answer. His family had driven around the terminal several times and walked the airport trying to find us. It was unbelievable! Finally, his oldest sister, Tina, located us at the baggage claim. When Clarence saw her, he sarcastically said, "Here comes the preacher." "Be nice, babe. It's been too long. Just let it go." His sister was a voluptuous girl. She seemed pleasant, but her voice was authoritative. They said hello to each other, and I thought, wait, they hadn't seen each other in many years, and this was a simple hello. What happened to the hugs and kisses? OMG, I can't believe it. Tina smiled and said, "Hi, Vanady." I responded, "Pleased to meet you, Tina." I was too afraid to go beyond that after what I had just witnessed.

The drive to Clarence's mother's house was quiet and hot. The greeting might have been a sign of something personal between them. Pulling up to the stucco house, family members greeted us outside. Okay, now this is much better. Everyone was so kind and happy to see Clarence. He was smiling, hugging, and exchanging dialogue with everyone. Now, this is what love is. It's what family is. It's what my parents taught me. Ms. Alexander had so much food prepared for us, and she even gave up her bedroom. She was trying so hard to make us feel welcome. We retired early because of jet lag and the three-hour time difference. We were worn out.

The next day was the Fourth of July, and the family had planned a barbecue. Clarence's dad was even coming in with his wife from Las Vegas. I was so excited to finally spend time with my husband and his family. I chose the cutest Capri jeans with white stars and a nice red sleeveless shirt to represent Independence Day. Clarence was up early, sitting at the kitchen table and talking to his mom. As I walked down the stairs, he said, "Here's my babe, and she can cook too, Mama." I blushed and responded, "Ms. Dina, your son is a good man to me and my children." She smiled, nodded, and abruptly got up to fix my plate. After the bountiful breakfast, the family started pouring in like ants in preparation for the big day. We laughed and played cards while the men grilled and drank liquor as early as noon. Tina was not happy about them drinking. She asked, "Why are they drinking anyway?" Clarence's other sister, Roberta, said, "Girl, everybody in this house knows the Lord. Don't start that judging stuff. Just let them enjoy themselves." Tina shouted, "You know how they act when they get too much in their system, especially Daddy and Clarence." I said, "Oh no, my Clarence can hold his own. He's good." Everyone looked at me dismayed, like, "If she only knew." I could not believe what I heard when one of the grandchildren yelled, "Mrs. Ora is sitting in the car with the A/C on, listening to music, and she won't get out." Roberta got up and headed toward the front door to bring Mrs. Ora Alexander, her stepmother, into the house. After about fifteen minutes, Tina went to the car to see what was taking so long. Meanwhile, Clarence came into the house from the backyard and lay a sweaty kiss on my lips. He smelled of liquor. "Babe," I said, "I believe you've had enough. Come sit with me for a minute." "Sit with you?" he slurred. "Vanady, I haven't seen my family in years, and you want me to sit with you! You know, it's just like you. You want all the darn attention all the time." "What did you just say, Clarence?" I was shocked at what I was hearing. "You heard every word I said, and I won't repeat myself; now leave me alone!" I was at a loss for words when he said those words. Roberta and Tina walked back into the house, shaking their heads, and saying, "That lady got issues." After hearing that, I got up and went outside to meet Mrs. Ora personally; besides, I needed some air. She rolled the window down as I waved to her. "Hi, Mrs. Ora. I'm Clarence's wife, Vanady." "Well, well… I finally get to meet the new Mrs. Alexander. Now tell me, how are you surviving those crazy folks in there?" I looked at her in shock at what had come out of her mouth. However, Mrs. Ora Alexander had a genuineness about her. I stayed outside and talked to her; over the next fifteen minutes, I learned quite a bit about the Alexander family. I was in awe at everything she said and how my husband treated me; I wanted to go home.

When I returned to the house, the guys were having a heated argument. Mrs. Dina was trying to intervene, begging them all to calm down. It was like mayhem had broken out in that entire house. I tried talking to Clarence, but he was so drunk and slurring curse words, calling everyone names, and disrespecting me and his mother with his unbelievable behavior. At that point, I'd had enough. Immediately, I ran upstairs and started packing. I was surrounded by evil, and I needed to get out. Clarence entered the bedroom, looked at me, and asked, "What are you doing? We got two more days here." "I can't take all of this, Clarence. Everyone is yelling and cursing, and no one has any respect for your mom or each other." "Vanady, periodically, we have gatherings that get a little out of hand. We always make up, babe." "I'm not used to this type of scene, Clarence, and how you have treated me is beyond disbelief. I have never seen you act in this manner towards me. What happened to the wonderful, caring man I fell in love with and married?" "I'm so sorry, babe. I had too much to drink. I promise things will be different from here on. Please, please stay with me. You're all that I have," he pleaded.

Things settled down the rest of the afternoon, and Clarence clung to me like Saran Wrap. The children popped their fireworks, and the adults sat around the table talking about old times. They talked about how Clarence quoted scriptures from the Bible and was a Sunday school scholar. They laughed at how he was able to walk through the Bloods' (red) territory and not be harmed because he was from the Crips' (blue) part of the projects and how brilliant he was at winning numerous academic awards. Clarence was their hope.

"If there is no struggle, there is no progress."

~**Frederick Douglass**~

~Chapter 13~

The warm shower felt great after that hot, humid roller-coaster ride on Independence Day and everything it entailed. Slipping into my cute two-piece lace bikini lingerie was sending a fiery signal to my husband. However, all I could hear was loud snoring, and I could smell him fumigating the room with gas from under the blanket. Darn, I need to relieve all this tension I'm feeling. These Alexander's got me jittery. I reached for my housecoat, put it on, and went downstairs to retrieve a glass of wine from the kitchen. As I was about to enter, I overheard Ms. Dina and Tina talking about Clarence and me. Tina said, "She seems to be nice. I wonder if she knows about Clarence?" Ms. Dina replied, "Well, maybe he's changed. He's never bought anyone home since his first wife." Tina laughed, saying, "I know nobody on this earth would put up with his evil ways, Mama." I let out a slight cough to let them know someone was approaching. "You guys still up?" I asked. "Yes," replied Ms. Dina. "We were talking about church tomorrow and how happy we are that you and Clarence will attend." "Oh yes, we go to church every Sunday, and sometimes I go twice." "That's good to hear, Vanady. Keep my brother under a covering," said Tina. "You know, it's funny you said that Tina, because Clarence says the same thing: I need to keep him in church." Ms. Dina and Tina looked at each other grimly as if they wanted to tell me something. "Okay, ladies, it's only us. What's going on with Clarence?" I asked. "Oh, nothing, baby," Ms. Dina said. "He's a changed man, I can tell." "What do you mean about changed, Ms. Dina?"

"No, he used to act out as a boy, getting into devilish little things. He's outgrown them. You have made my son so happy, and he adores you. Whatever you're doing, keep doing it. That's in the past." "Thank you, ma'am. He makes me happy, and we complement each other. Now, I need a little red wine to relax me. Do you have any?" "Of course, I will join you."

Ms. Dina handed me a clear plastic cup, and I said, "I apologize, but I can only drink wine from a glass. It's a habit." "Oh, no problem. I will get one out of my China cabinet just for you," she laughed. "Thank you, Ms. Dina! How about you, Tina? Will you join us?" "Who, me? Drinking is a sin." "What do you mean a sin? Didn't Jesus turn water into wine? So, you call Him a sinner, too?" "No, that's not what I'm saying. Like my brothers and Daddy did earlier, people take things out of context and become drunkards." "Well, as you can see, your mother and I are having a friendly glass of wine to relax us. Now, is that a sin? Secondly, I don't drink to get drunk. I have a glass a few times a week or so, and while you're on that note, I also like to dance. Don't you know the story of David and how he danced? Is dancing considered a sin, too, Tina?" "Well, Vanady, I don't know if you're being sarcastic or what, but it doesn't make any difference. You have your beliefs, and I have mine. You will find out sooner or later, Mrs. Clarence Alexander!" Tina stated as she stormed out of the room.
"OMG! Where did all that come from, Ms. Dina? Is there something about my husband that I need to know?" "No, Vanady, those two never got along as kids. She has to learn how to forgive and forget." "It's okay. I like Tina and can tell she loves the Lord like I do."

Later, as I eased into bed, Clarence's back was turned away from me. He was acting strange. All of a sudden, out of nowhere, the television turned on.

I shook Clarence and whispered, "Babe, do you have the remote control, and did you mistakenly turn the television on?" "No, that television doesn't have a remote. Go to sleep, Vanady," he replied.

Those words were not good enough for me, so I got out of bed and manually turned the television off. The darn thing turned on as soon as I slipped back into bed. This is creepy, I thought as I moved closer to him shaking in my boots under the covers. Unable to sleep with the television on, I got up to find the cord to unplug the television from the wall outlet. Okay, God, maybe now I can get some rest.

Falling into a deep sleep, I dreamed of dark, evil things, which awakened me to see an electric blue line running across the television screen. "Darn! What the hell is this?" The air in that bedroom was so warm and thick, and to top it off, Clarence was talking in his sleep and making weird sounds. I was scared stiff.

The following day, we ate an early breakfast and prepared for worship service at Tina's church. Clarence didn't want to go, but I insisted. He thought Tina was a hypocrite and too judgmental. Once we reached the small church, Tina was in full effect, fulfilling her duties. The preacher talked about individuals who smiled in your face but had a dagger in your back. He called them "backstabbers." I asked Clarence, "Doesn't that sound like the lady at your job that you always complain about, Andrea?" He just looked at me with the evilest look on his face. I said, "Are you okay, babe?" He looked the other way and didn't respond.

After service let out, I stood with Ms. Dina, meeting Tina's friends and her pastor, while Clarence chose to sit in the car and wait. Once Ms. Dina and I got into the car, I said, "Clarence, it was rude of you not to shake Tina's pastor's hand, at least."

He harshly replied, "That pastor is the biggest phony in Los Angeles. He's a money-hungry podium pimp!" "Stop it, Clarence! Don't talk like that in front of your mama. That's just plain rude." "Oh, you haven't seen rude yet!" I was floored! This was not the man I'd just married. Who is this stranger? Tomorrow morning, It can't get here fast enough; I must leave this house!

Clarence did not talk to me and his mother for the rest of the day. I was so hurt and bewildered that I felt numb. As I packed that evening, Clarence grumbled, "Don't touch my stuff." "What did you say, Clarence?" "I said, don't touch my stuff!" Stunned, I ran downstairs to find his mother and get some answers for his deplorable behavior. Ms. Dina was sitting quietly by the window, staring into the dark. "Ma'am, may I talk to you briefly, please?" I asked. "Sit, child," she said. "My son is a special person. He had difficulty growing up and experienced things normal children don't. He is a good man, Vanady, but he is just confused about right and wrong. You are a sweet, loving young lady, but I need you to do something for me and your marriage. When you get him back home, take him to get some help. Promise me?" she pleaded. "God help me," I whispered. What have I done... again?

"Misery won't touch you gentle.

It always leaves its thumbprints on you;

sometimes it leaves them for others to see,

sometimes for nobody but you to know of."

~Edwidge Danticat~

~Chapter 14~

The plane ride from California to Florida will forever resonate in my soul. My husband did not help carry my luggage, and he requested a different seat on the airplane away from me. I was so heartbroken. As he laughed and shared in dialogue with the Caucasian young woman sitting next to him, I wore a face of humiliation. It's only been two months; I could get an annulment as Samantha's mama suggested. This guy is a Dr. Jekyll and Mr. Hyde.

When we exited the plane in Fort Lauderdale, Clarence never looked my way. He even stood on the other side of the baggage claim ramp. After grabbing his luggage, he walked swiftly towards the parking garage exit. God, if this man leaves me in this airport, I promise he will regret it for the rest of his life. I have had enough, Father. As I reached the vehicle with luggage in hand, I saw that the idiot had already put his belongings in and was sitting quietly in the driver's seat. I calmly opened the hatch and put my luggage in. Then I closed the hatch, got into the passenger's side front seat, and didn't say a word to Mr. Clarence Alexander all the way home.

When we pulled into the driveway, I hit the garage door opener, exited the vehicle, opened the hatch, and took my belongings out. I walked into the house, leaving my luggage in the downstairs family room, and immediately watered my plants. I went upstairs, took a shower, and pretended Mr. Clarence Alexander never existed. Later on, as I was fixing myself a sandwich, he came downstairs, grabbed his keys off the countertop, never mumbled a word, and left. I was so relieved. I needed to eat first and then cry and think about what I would do about my life.

Lying down that night, my sleep was off balance due to the time zone difference in California. But I had a ram in the bush; I had been saving the Tylenol PM for a special occasion like this. It was after one am when I felt the mattress go down on the other side of the king-size bed. I turned over and went back to sleep. Around three am, I was shockingly awakened to find Clarence on his knees in the back of me, sniffing up and down my back and making doglike sounds. I jumped out of the bed and said, "What are you doing?" It was like he was in a trance. Never responding, Clarence laid back down and quickly fell asleep. What in the hell just happened? I wondered. Unable to sleep, I went downstairs and made hot tea. My mind was going a million miles a minute. I was baffled.

The following day, Clarence got up and walked out the door without even mumbling a word. I was weary from the night before, from sleep deprivation, and had planned on sitting in my warm bath and crying my eyes out with the hope it would get rid of the pain. The old phrase "Crying cleanses the soul" obviously wasn't working for me. So, in my nakedness, I fell across the bed and allowed the floodgates to open. As the tears and saliva met in the center of my pillow, I cried, "Why me, Lord?" Finally, I returned to bed to catch up on some much-needed rest.

It was after noon when my cell phone rang. Samantha wanted to do lunch, and I needed to vent to my best friend. We met at a nearby restaurant, and my hand was shaking when I handed her the souvenir I had bought for her from the Chinese market in Los Angeles.

"Girl, what's wrong with you? You look like you've been to hell and back. And why are you acting so nervous like that?" "Samantha, I messed up. I don't have any idea who this man is. I married." "Vanady, I told you to wait. There was something about him I just couldn't put my finger on. Girl, what did he do to you?" "It's crazy, Samantha. I discern an eerie, almost evil presence in him. I am still determining what it is. I must pray harder because this is getting the best of me." "Well, you've only been married for a couple of months. Do you know you can still get an annulment?" "I know, Samantha, but I must wait for God's answer; I am so confused and heartbroken. I never thought I would feel this way again. I'm such a fool." "No, you're not. You just married an unequally yoked nutcase." "Girl, you are too funny, but you are right! Okay, let's have a drink and toast to Crazy Clarence! Woo Hoo!"

"Change will not come

if we wait for some other person

or some other time.

We are the ones we've been waiting for.

We are the change that we seek."

~President Barack Obama~

~Chapter 15~

My first day back in the office was like walking into a whirlwind; everything was scattered in piles, but it felt good to be needed again. Clarence and I have been doing poorly since the California trip. However, duty called, and I needed to thrust myself into my workload to forget my whole life for the time being. Mr. Gillian's book was finally ready to go to print. Greta had called him to tell him the good news, and he stopped by with lunch for the entire staff. I love to see the expressions on my authors faces when they get news such as this. It turned out to be a busy but productive day. Thank God my kids were away for the summer and wouldn't have to witness what happened in our home.

I decided to talk to Clarence about everything, win or lose, that evening. I cooked pork chops, broccoli with cheese, and candied yams. It was one of his favorite meals. He took forever to get home, but I waited patiently, keeping the food warm. When he walked in the door, the food hit his nostrils. Surprisingly, he said, "Good evening." I said, "Hi, are you ready to eat?" "Of course, babe. I'm starving."

After we ate dinner, I offered him a drink, and he obliged. "May we talk for a little bit, Clarence?" "Go ahead, Vanady. The floor is yours." "What happened to us? Ever since we went to visit your family in California, something has drastically changed. You act as if I did something to you. You treat me as if I don't exist. You show me no love. What have I done to deserve all this, Clarence?"

"Vanady, I can't explain it. Something comes over me, babe, and I say and do things I know are wrong. I try to control it, but it's too powerful. That's why I told you before we married about those voices in my head telling me to do evil things. You thought I was kidding. I told you all that for a reason, so that you can help me. I never admitted anything about myself until I met and fell in love with you. I just dismissed it and moved on to the next. I love you like no other woman, but sometimes, babe, it takes over," he vented. "Have you prayed and asked God to help you, Clarence?" "Vanady, I have prayed so much about this thing until I've run out of words. Will you please help me, babe? I know you're a real woman of God. You can get a prayer through to heaven for me. I hear you when you are praying at night." Clarence was crying out for help. "Of course, I will help you, sweetheart, but we must agree and be in accord. It's called Spiritual Warfare, Clarence; that's what we're going through. When it affects you, it affects me because I am your wife. It's obvious the enemy wants something from you or wants you to stop doing something you're doing. Clarence, together we're strong, but divided, we fall. We are in for a fight, but God has equipped us with weaponry." "What do you mean by weaponry, babe?" "The Bible is your sword. Nothing can stand up against His Word," I said, trying to encourage him. "He has given us the helmet of salvation to cover our minds, the breastplate of righteousness to shield our hearts, and sandals to guide our walk. So, you see, we are not alone in this; the Holy Spirit and the angels are watching and interceding on our behalf. I knew from my childhood that I was called to do something special for God." "So did I!" Clarence said excitedly.

"Well, babe, it's not going to be easy. The enemy comes to steal, kill, and destroy, and we've been put on his hit list." Surprisingly, Clarence grabbed me and said, "Would you pray for us?" I began the prayer by thanking God for all that He had done and was doing in our lives. I thanked Him for our health, families, and loved ones. I asked God to cover and regulate our minds so we would think thoughts of Him in our daily lives. I pleaded for the blood of Jesus to come over our home, finances, children, marriage, jobs, and our day-to-day walk. I rebuked the enemy and told him he had no right in our household, marriage, or any area of our lives. I told that nasty scoundrel that he would take his filthy hands off of my husband's mind, and by the Holy Ghost Fire, I would take the authority to send him and every one of his evil spirits, imps, warlocks, witches, etc., back to Hell! I called on my help, sanctioning Michael, Gabriel, and a host of angels to stand with flaming swords on the four corners of our home to strike down anything that was not of God that tried to come near it. I prayed for strength and wisdom as we faced our day-to-day. I sealed the prayer by thanking God for victory and for what was already done. Clarence had tears in his eyes. I said, "No time for tears; we are at war. However, victory is ours. Now let's rejoice in the Holy Spirit!"

"Hate is too great a burden to bear.

It injures the hater

more than it injures the hated."

~Coretta Scott King~

~Chapter 16~

The next few weeks went by swiftly, with Clarence and me getting along very well, considering all the craziness that had taken place in California. He was attentive and affectionate, and we discussed him purchasing me a brand-new Mercedes-Benz. Excitement was in the air because my son and daughter were returning from summer vacations with extended family. We fired up the grill, making ribs, chicken, and hamburgers. I also made my famous shrimp and rice, accompanied by baked beans and sweet corn on the cob. The children were so happy to return home that evening that they talked Clarence's and my ears off. Victor was headed into his last year of high school, and Vanessa was in the fourth grade. Overall, they were great kids. The next day, Vanessa and I went to Publix to purchase groceries for the week and Sunday's dinner. When we returned, I hit the button on the remote to the garage door opener. But as the door rose, all I could see inside the garage was swinging arms. "What the hell!" I parked the car and jumped out of it with the engine still running. "What's going on?" I yelled. Victor yelled back, "He called me a sorry motherf'er!" "Clarence, what happened?" I yelled! "Vanady, I told him to wash the darn dishes, and he said, 'I'm busy, and I will do them when I feel like it and you don't tell me what to do. You ain't my Daddy.'" Victor yelled back, "Mama, he's lying; I was minding my own business, making some beats on my keyboard, when he burst into my bedroom telling me to get my lazy behind downstairs and wash the dishes. He tried to punk me, Mama! I told him I was almost finished and would do them then. He yelled, 'Get your mother f'in butt downstairs now and do them!' Yes, Mama, I said 'F you!' Then he pushed me, and I defended myself by pushing him back. I tried to get away from him, but he kept coming after me like some crazy lunatic, following me into the garage. Mama, I swear he's crazy! I'm not just going to stand by and allow him to push and punch me. I ain't no punk!" "Vanady, he's lying!" Clarence yelled. "Okay! I have heard enough!" I shouted. "The both of you need to calm the hell down! I can't take it! You guys are about to drive me crazy! I'm your mother, Victor, and yes, Clarence, I am your wife, so please tell me what you are trying to do to me. Break my heart?" "Mama, I promise I was minding my own business." "Shut up, Victor! I don't need to hear anything from either of you right now! Victor and Vanessa, take these groceries into the house, and Clarence, I need to speak with you upstairs."

Once we were alone in the bedroom, I turned to Clarence and said, "Tell me, why would you wait until I left the house for thirty minutes to approach Victor about the dishes? You never said a mumbling word about the dishes while I was here. What triggered you to tell him he needed to do them now, Clarence?" "Well, babe, I was sitting there watching TV, and I started to think about how hard you and I work, and he's up there just making music on that loud keyboard. He needed to do something other than bang on that thing all day. So, I wanted to surprise you by having the kitchen clean and everything in place when you and Vanessa came home from the grocery store. Babe, I swear I was trying to do the right thing." "Okay, Clarence, why did you have to put your hands on him?" "Well, he was puffing up at me like he wanted to move something, and I had to show him who the man of this house is." "I am surprised at you," I said with disappointment. "Victor will be eighteen years old in a few months. He's a man. He won't let you or anyone push or punch him and not retaliate. You should have waited on me, and I would have handled everything." "I'm sorry, Vanady; he pushed me to the edge." "Listen, Clarence, that's my son. Neither you nor anyone else has the right to attack him physically. I will deal with him about his behavior, but you need to check yourself too."

I was torn, stuck between a rock and a hard place. Inside, I was crying and confused. "God, please help me," I prayed aloud. "I am a mother, and I am a wife. What do I do?" Walking down the stairs, I noticed Victor standing at the sink and washing the dishes. "Mama, I promise I don't know what's wrong with him. He attacked me. There is something evil about that man; he fooled all of us. I promise I will take him out if he comes after me again, Mama!" "Listen, Victor, don't talk like that. I need help understanding a lot. I'm waiting on God. I need you to trust me on this."

Looking at my only son as he washed the dishes, I could see the hurt, frustration, and anger that had swelled up in him. I didn't want him to feel I was choosing sides; I needed him to give me time to sort through all the mayhem. I needed him to forgive Clarence. Later that night, as I sat in the family room alone, I reflected on my life and the choices that I had made. I messed up this time, Father, I pleaded. "Okay, Vanady. Shake it off. There will be no more 'woe me' moments. **Stand, Woman, Stand!**" a voice whispered.

When I got in the bed, something felt unusual lying next to Clarence that night. I couldn't figure out the thickness of the unsettling air in our bedroom. Hey, what's going on? I asked myself. Is the air vent blowing directly on my thighs, or is it these silk pajamas I am wearing? No, this is strange, almost eerie. As I felt the touches up and down my legs and thighs, I asked myself, girl, have you finally lost it? Whoa, this is not funny because my husband is asleep on the opposite side of the bed, so if he's over there, and the air conditioning is not on, who is touching me? God, am I going crazy? I can't tell anybody about this; they'll probably have me committed.

Night after night, the touches returned; I didn't know what to do, so I succumbed and confided in a spiritual friend, who told me that I was not losing it. He explained that when God is taking you higher, and a call has been placed on your life, the enemy will try to place fear and do anything to stop you from walking into destiny. He then stated, "Next time it happens, speak out loud the name of the Father, plead the blood, and rebuke every unclean spirit back to the pits of Hell." Lastly, he told me that the price had already been paid and to anoint my house and myself every night. I followed his instructions the next day and couldn't believe how quickly it worked! Thank you, God, for your help!

"For I am my mother's daughter,

and the drums of Africa still beat in my heart."

~Mary McLeod Bethune~

~Chapter 17~

God had been dealing with me about reaching out to women who needed support, whether it was spiritual, emotional, psychological, physical, or just issues of life. I prayed and asked God for guidance on how to help these broken, battered, abused, neglected, rejected, confused, hurting women. I needed an objective, a mission statement, a name for the women's group, and individuals who would support me in giving birth to it. The very first thing He whispered into my spirit was, "Women Answering the Call." Wow! That was quick. Okay, God, I like the name. Now, when, and where do I begin?

It would take me three months to organize, plan, and follow the mandate that had been placed on my life for the manifestation of W.A.C. (Women Answering the Call). On August 8, 2006, W.A.C would have its first meeting in my sister Lolita's living room, attended by eight women. God was doing a new thing in my life. Every other Thursday evening, we gathered to share, uplift, motivate, empower, and pray for one another. Within a few months, there were so many women attending that we could barely fit into Lolita's home anymore; W.A.C. was bursting at the seams. I prayed for provision for the vision and for God to open the doors to a larger venue so no one would be turned away. Something was happening to these women as they were being inspired through the word of God. As they shared their stories and testimonies, they were being delivered, changed, and set free from substance abuse, alcoholism, prostitution, stripping, etc. Every meeting, someone gave their life over to God; they were coming into their own. My greatest joy was witnessing them falling in love with Jesus Christ and His Word. Eventually, W.A.C. meetings relocated to a larger venue, a nearby hotel conference room. Thank you, God, for what you have entrusted to me! I'd known since childhood that I would do something special for God one day. I was sold out for Him, and I was proud of the woman of God that I was evolving into. I was finally walking into destiny and discovering my purpose. However, when the praise, prayer, and worship was over, and I returned home, there was always a negative spirit waiting for me. By this time, it didn't matter anymore how Clarence felt about God and me; I was not going to allow him to ruin the relationship I had with my Heavenly Father. God was working in me, and since Clarence's coldness couldn't shake me the way it used to… I was standing my ground. Truth be told, there was still a struggle at home when the lights went out every night.

As I popped my Tylenol PM and swallowed the measured cup of Nyquil to help me sleep, I thought, Vanady, this is so sad. You have allowed your life to be reduced to this over-the-counter medication for a decent night of rest. Reaching for my companions: the anointing oil, which helped me to fight off demonic forces, and my Bible (which I slept with under my pillow), I had no idea what that particular night would entail. For some reason, the sleep-aids always worked very quickly on me, and I let out a big yawn before closing my eyes. Squirming to get into my best spoon position, I turned towards Clarence on the opposite side of the bed and noticed the numbers on the analog clock that read, one eleven am. I thought, Okay, God, one is for the Father, one for the Son, and one for the Holy Spirit. With those numbers, I'm sure to get a great night's sleep tonight. Thank you, God!

Before my first snore, though, the phone rang, startling me out of my drowsy sleep. Turning over, I looked at the caller ID on the house phone and noticed the California area code. Father, please let everything be okay. I am so at my breaking point, I pleaded. Saying hello, I didn't recognize the timid voice on the other end of the phone. But when she identified herself as Clarence's daughter, I sat straight up in the bed. He had been estranged from all three of his kids for some time now. Of course, he'd never shared any of this prior to our marriage, except to tell me that his daughter hung out with the wrong crowd and chose not to allow him into her life, coupled with child support issues with her mother. The mother of his other two biracial children refused to have any type of relationship with him because of child support and a very nasty divorce. I was beginning to realize how naive and gullible I'd been in those days when we'd first met. God, if only I had done my homework and waited on you, I wouldn't be in this mess right now.

The voice blubbered, "May I speak to my daddy?" "Who is this?" I asked. "I'm Kamirah." "Hi, Kamirah, this is your dad's wife, Vanady. Is everything okay?" "Will you please just put my daddy on the phone, Mrs. Vanady. It's an emergency." I wanted to say, "Excuse me?" but I kept my composure and called out to sleeping Clarence. "Babe, your daughter Kamirah is on the phone. It sounds like something important. She needs to speak with you." "Who is on the phone?" he asked. "Your daughter Kamirah and it's an emergency." "Why is she calling my house?" Clarence blurted out. "Guy, this is your baby. She says it's an emergency. Now talk to her." "Vanady, leave me the hell alone! Don't you see I'm trying to sleep?" Oh God, I prayed, please help me. I'm so sleepy and irrational right now. Give me the words to say to this child. I don't have time for this. Returning to the phone,

I explained to Kamirah that her dad had had a long day and would return her call tomorrow. "Mrs. Vanady, all I wanted to do was tell him they found a tumor on my brain, and it might be cancerous. I'm having brain surgery tomorrow morning, and I wanted to tell him that I love him and say goodbye in case I don't make it. "Kamirah, you will make it! Don't ever say those words again, you hear me! We serve an awesome God who is a Healer, and you are going to be alright. Hold on, Kamirah, for a minute. I'm going to wake him up," I told her. Placing the phone on mute so Kamirah wouldn't hear, I yelled, "Clarence! Clarence! I know you hear me. Enough is enough! Now, that's your blood. That's your child who's facing major surgery tomorrow. She just wants to hear your voice. Will you please get on the phone?" For a moment there was silence, but then he grudgingly said, "Vanady, tell that girl to not ever call my house again!" "Clarence, did you hear what I just said? She's sick with a potentially cancerous brain tumor. Please take the phone," I begged. "Listen, Vanady, I don't do those people. If she was in the middle of the street dying and needed a sip of water to survive, I would walk by her and smile." "What in the hell did you just say?" "You heard me, Vanady; she is dead to me, just like the others!"

Oh God, please! This is too much; I can't believe what just came out of this mother f'ers mouth! I need you to touch me, God, because that old nature is trying to come forth. That old Vanady died; please don't allow her to resurrect, because I'm about to cuss him out! "Clarence!" "Leave me the hell alone, Vanady! This is none of your business. Stay out of it!" "Dude, what the hell do you mean, 'stay out of it'?" Clarence grumbled something, placed the pillow over his head, and let out a stink bomb, which was his way of saying, "You ain't shitz."

My God, my Strength, my Redeemer, what do I say to this child? Help me, please! Returning to the phone, I know that my mouth was just the instrument, because the Holy Spirit had taken over. "Kamirah, listen. I need you to hear me out. I don't care what the doctor said, nor do I care what the chart or x-rays read. YOU ARE HEALED! I need you to believe and receive those words right now! Do you hear me, Kamirah!"

"But, Mrs. Vanady, I only wanted to say good-bye." She then hung up the phone, breaking another piece off my shattered heart. Silence like never before filled my bedroom as I wept for my unknown, distant stepdaughter... who was facing a life and death situation and whose biological father couldn't care less.

Sitting on the floor with my back against the bed's footboard, I felt like the servant Job as I cried out, stripping myself of every piece of clothing down to even my underwear. As I lay naked with my face buried into the bedroom floors carpet, I prayed, Father God, please in the name of your Son, hear my plea. This child didn't ask to come into this world. It wasn't her fault what happened between Clarence and her mother. Father, I know you have the power to say yes or no. Please, I beg, Heavenly Father, extend your Mercy and Grace towards Kamirah and her parents. I know you are a forgiving God, and I know there is nothing too hard for You! Heal her, Lord! Raise her up out of this situation! Breathe on her and restore her back to good health! Lord, show Kamirah and the world how GREAT Thou are! Someway, somehow, let Kamirah know that I tried everything that I could to get her daddy to talk to her tonight. However, when it's all said and done, you are that Father she really needed to talk to and have the final say with! I seal this prayer, believing and receiving.

"Never underestimate the power and the influence of the human spirit. We are all the same in this notion: The potential for greatness lives within each of us."

~Wilma Rudolph~

~Chapter 18~

As my relationship with God grew, trouble in my home brewed, too. But something strange happened to me in the month when I'd spoken with my stepdaughter Kamirah for the first time. I started to feel like giving up on the marriage. I was traumatized. Clarence had no idea I had been communicating with Kamiah's mother since that dreadful night. My stepdaughter's surgery had gone well, and the tumor on her brain was benign. She was now back in school and doing fine, a fact that her mother happily shared with me in our last conversation confirmed how God is so amazing and powerful!

Despite how Clarence was treating me and the emotional state I was in, I refused to let go of the relationship that I had discovered with the Lord. All of my life, I'd desired true love with no strings attached. I'd wanted to be loved for Vanady. From my inner to my outer being, I'd craved that unspeakable joy and that peace that would calm all the unsettled winds in my life. An "agape" love was what I'd longed for, and I had finally found it in the Lord, and no one was going to take that away! I didn't understand what warfare was until I gave my life to Jesus Christ. The fight between carnality and spirituality was a war within itself in every area of my life.

"Why is it so hard serving Him?" I would ask the assistant pastor at the church. He would pray with me and share Jesus's crucifixion and resurrection. He would also give me scriptures to read and that special oil I used to anoint my home. I was progressing in my walk with Christ. Every day, I became stronger and wiser.

Clarence was jealous of the assistant pastor, who counseled and prayed regularly with me. He was also envious of any preacher, TV evangelist, and even the Bible itself. He clarified it by hiding my Bibles and television remote controls, unplugging phone lines, etc. Clarence was jealous of God.

Strange things were happening in my home: creepy, eerie things. In the beginning, I thought, once I give my life to the Lord, everything will be all right. However, if anything, it was the total opposite. It felt like I was living in hell right here on earth. The Bible says, "Obedience is better than sacrifice." With all of my weaponry, it still seemed as though this situation was getting the best of me as I tried to obey God's commandments. It seemed the harder I prayed, the more intense the warfare became. Some days, I stayed on my knees, praying until they were bruised and bloody. What's worse is that I couldn't share what I was going through with my family; Samantha and a small circle of prayer warriors from church were the only ones I could trust. I have heard the saying, "God sends people in your life for seasons, reasons, and lifetimes." Now, I could honestly say I understood that phrase.

Pastor Richardson was on my phones speed dial, and Clarence detested him and Samantha. Whenever I announced that I was going to church for eleven a.m. worship, he would become very argumentative and say ungodly things about the church and its leadership.

Astoundingly, though, Clarence would awaken at six am most Sundays, and I would attend his church with him for seven thirty am worship. The pastor was one of the country's greatest gospel proclaimers in the United States. Dr. Carterson was a teacher and anointed man of God known for his brilliance and humility. Clarence liked him and enjoyed his sermons. However, Clarence refused to put one dollar in the offering when the ushers passed the collection basket. He would get upset with me when I would fill out an envelope and place my check inside. Most times, I would fill out an envelope on his behalf because I was embarrassed, as the ushers noticed his stance on not touching the basket Sunday after Sunday. He was adamant and didn't believe in giving anything to the church or any religious/spiritual entity. I questioned him about how he thought the church was supposed to maintain itself without money for electricity, water, maintenance, shelter, or help for the destitute, etc. He would say, "Jesus didn't need a building; He stood on top of rocks and dirt and even preached from the water." He felt all preachers were out for only one thing: money! Clarence clarified that he would not spend a penny of his on their homes, luxury cars, and women.

I found it almost unbelievable that Clarence could be so intrigued with the sermon, which usually exposed him, but he was in total denial about it having anything to do with him. During the sermon, he would nod his head and pat his feet, and at home, he would talk about how the pastor's sermon touched and enlightened him. Trust me, it lasted only a day or two, and then he returned to Dr. Jekyll and Mr. Hyde.

The closer I got to God, the more my husband rebelled against God and me. One day, after work, as I pulled into the carport, to my surprise, Clarence was standing behind his SUV with a box in his hands. Oh no, not again, I thought. Please, God, not another one. He promised he would be nicer to his employees this time. He promised he would be a team player. Father, what's wrong with him? Is he so blind that he can't see he's being used repeatedly by the enemy? I know he's not a people person, but that job had great benefits, bonuses, and advancement opportunities. God, will the blinders ever come off? Will he ever look at the man in the mirror and realize he is the problem instead of the world?

The sad thing was that he was never fired for job performance; his recluse demeanor affected him so negatively. He would walk around boasting, "I'm a one-person team that doesn't need input or help from anyone. I'll do it my way, or they can hit the highway." Lord, here we are, living in this big two-story house with a brand-new Mercedes-Benz and SUV, with monthly payments that need to be made. How can a person be fired four times in two and a half years? Can somebody tell me? Please, God, put a muzzle on my mouth because I have had about enough of him and his self-centered ways and childlike demeanor. He is one arrogant piece of shitz!

Clarence walked over to my car and said, "Babe, I don't know what happened. I didn't do anything this time. They just told me they were letting me go," he pleaded. "Vanady, I tried to get along with everyone this time. I was a team player like you told me to be. I don't understand what I did wrong." Okay, God. Give me the words to say to this man right about now. You increase and decrease me because my cup has run over.

Once inside, Clarence went straight to the cabinet, grabbed the bottle of Hennessey, and filled the six-ounce glass to the rim with a few ice cubes, straight up. God was doing something new in my life as I moved silently to prepare dinner.

"Vanady, we're going to be all right, babe. I know of at least a dozen engineering companies that are interested in me right now. Those guys are going to be sorry they let me go. I'll show them." As I stirred the spaghetti sauce, I was listening but not listening. Clarence was already on the phone with the headhunter from Southern Fork Construction, sharing his salary requirements and benefits. When I finished cooking dinner, he was on his second glass of Hennessey. One good thing I must say about Clarence Alexander was that he was very kindhearted towards me when he became drunk. "Vanady, babe," he slurred, "I love you, girl. I got the best wife in the world with your fine azz."

"Come sit at the table and eat with me, Clarence," I said. "Okay, just a small plate, baby. I don't have much of an appetite tonight." As we sat and ate together, he seemed to be amused at what his day had entailed. God, he just doesn't get it, I thought. After showering, I prepared to read the Bible before bed and noticed he wasn't there. I discovered him crying as I crept and peeped around the staircase corner wall. My demanding "I don't need anybody" husband was exposed today. He does cry real tears. He hurts like me. He's HUMAN! Inhaling and then exhaling, I walked over to Clarence and told him it would be all right as I hugged him tightly.

While comforting him, I was shocked at his following statement. This fool said, "God will deal with all the people who fired me over the years." He then talked about how much he loved God and his family and how he would serve God faithfully from this day forth. Of course, I listened, but I was tired of repeatedly hearing that same old story. Honestly, what I wanted to say was, "Shut the hell up, you hypocrite! You don't care about anything or anyone but yourself. When you're on top of the world, God is almost non-existent. But every time you lose a job, or your money gets funny, it's all about God and family. You're such a fraud, Clarence Alexander!" Boy, I couldn't wait until I could say those words. Forgive me, Father, if I seem insensitive, but I'm tired of his shitz!

As the caring wife, I grabbed his hand to lead him upstairs to bed, but he rejected me and said he would be up later. Father, I need a relevant word tonight. I need to understand what is happening in my home, husband, marriage, and life.

As I perused the King James Bible, I was led to chapter 27 of the Book of Psalms. Although I had read that chapter many times, tonight, it was as if it had been written personally for me. As the words leaped off the pages into my spirit, verse 14 overtook me. It read: "Wait on the Lord; be of good courage, and he shall strengthen thine heart; wait, I say, on the Lord."

"I hear you, Father," I whispered. As I knelt at the side of the bed, I reached for the anointing oil and poured some into my hand. Then I covered myself from the top of my head to the soles of my feet as I prayed aloud, "Father, forgive me of my sins known and unknown, cleanse me from all unrighteousness, be the light upon my feet, and cover me in Your blood. God, I know your grace is sufficient, so please have mercy on me. I'm so weary, Lord. You say you will be my burden bearer and heavy load sharer… Please save my family. Please rescue me!"

"The greatest lie ever told about love is that it sets you free."

~Zadie Smith~

~Chapter 19~

My dreams and visions had become very vivid over the last few months. I felt God was trying to tell me something. However, Clarence had gotten on with a major construction company with an excellent salary, like his last job, with bonuses. He was back to being Mr. Egotistical as if he were invincible. Every day was an adventure in my household... You never knew what to expect. My son, Victor, stayed out of Clarence's way, but Clarence adored my baby girl, Vanessa. He'd shower her with lovely presents and monetary gifts periodically. Clarence was drinking very heavily; he was what they call a functioning alcoholic. He never missed a day of work and brought every problem and situation home daily. He was driving me up the wall!

Money and status ruled him. One day, he said, "Vanady, you are an exception to the rule, but only because I love you. Anyone who doesn't make six figures is not on my level." "Don't say that, Clarence. We have family and friends who don't make that type of money. Please don't ever say that again." "Whatever," he said arrogantly. Sorting through the mail later that evening, my heart stopped. Oh my God, we have a final notice on the electricity bill. Oh God! How could I have been so stupid as to miss putting this in the budget? Clarence is going to have a hissy fit! I'll tell him to leave a blank check on the dining room table from the household account and hope he doesn't ask for the bill.

The following day at six am, he screamed my name, "Vanady!" Lethargically, I said, "Yes, babe, you called me?" "What the Hell is this? Come down here, right now!" Not being a morning person, I asked, "What do you want?" "Come here! You need to explain this!" I don't know what came over me, but it had to be Roe. I slipped out of bed, dressed in my black Fredrick's of Hollywood short negligee, and sat on the top stair of the staircase. I uncaringly said, "What do you want, Clarence? I'm sleepy." "What the hell is this, Vanady?" Surprised, I asked, "What are you talking about, Clarence?" "This darn electric bill that has a final notice, that's what I'm talking about. You know I don't play regarding late fees and my credit. Why didn't you tell me about this? Darn, can't you do anything right?" he yelled. "I apologize, Clarence, but I have had a lot on my plate lately with my daddy and my sister being sick with breast cancer. It slipped my mind, babe." "That's not good enough, Vanady. You are always making excuses for being who you are!" "And what am I, Clarence?" He hissed, "Take a look in the mirror and ask yourself the question! Yeah, that's what you need to do, Miss Godly!" My grandma always said, "Pick and choose your battles." I was not about to let this inconsiderate bastard ruin my day, so I just walked away.

Upon Clarence's arrival, I spoke and offered him dinner that evening. He looked at me as if I was the scum of the earth, opened the refrigerator, grabbed a beer, and went upstairs without speaking. OMG! This man is trying my last nerve, God; place a bridle on my mouth. Something had happened to my husband since he'd gotten this new job. Yes, he was very arrogant, but I noticed a dark side that seemed to darken daily. Clarence looked at me as if he detested me, and he had not spoken to me for over a week since the electric bill incident. He was full of himself and felt he didn't need anybody. The harder I prayed and tried to talk to him, the more he rejected me. I had never, ever, in my entire life been so mistreated. This was new territory for me. I didn't want to be a divorce statistic—again—so I vowed to God and myself that no matter what, I was going to save my husband and my marriage.

In the meantime, my relationship with God was continuously developing. I was maturing in His word, and my prayers had become more powerful, meaningful, and moving. If my husband had done anything positive for me with his nasty disposition, he'd pushed me to my knees like never before. But even more importantly, I was discovering my spiritual gifts. In the beginning, I was afraid and uncertain about myself. I couldn't understand how God could use someone like me with such a blemished past. However, as I read His word and discovered others who had fallen short, and even how a murderer named Saul had been used to share the Gospel with many, it gave me newfound hope for myself. Suddenly, through church and Women Answering the Call Ministries, people called me to pray for them and their loved ones. My phone rang constantly, placing Clarence in a panicked state. "You all are a bunch of hypocrites!" he yelled at me one night. "You so-called Christians are the worst people on this damn planet. Every last one of you is going straight to Hell! I didn't marry this woman here; I married someone else! Why have you got to be trying to save the world, Vanady? It's as if you have chosen them over me!" "No, Clarence, I chose God over you. Sweetheart, life is short, and tomorrow is not promised. We got to get it right if we want to please God." "What about pleasing me? All you talk about daily is your women's group, church, and God!" "No, Clarence. I just want us to be happy by loving God first and then each other. You are who you are, I am who I am, and we are one. We took a vow, and I don't know about you, but I plan on standing by it." "Vanady! Stop trying to save something that doesn't want to be saved!"

"What did you say, Clarence?" "You heard me! Leave me the Hell alone!" "What do you want from me, Clarence?" "I don't want to hear all this religious crap, Vanady. Keep it out of this house." "Clarence, first of all, I'm not religious. I am a spiritual being who loves the Lord and will do anything He asks of me. Secondly, it's okay for you to bring your job home with you every evening and drink your issues away. Here, I am fulfilling all my wifely duties and praying for my family. What's wrong with that, Clarence?" "You are getting on my last freaking nerve, Vanady, and you're about to get a good old-fashioned cursing out. Now, shut the Hell up! I don't want to hear that crap every darn day!"

Clarence didn't speak to me the rest of that evening. On my knees that night, I petitioned God for help because I loved my husband, and I loved the institution of marriage, but how much more could any human being take? Tossing and turning that night, the clock read three thirty am, and I didn't feel sleepy. As I lay there, I stared at Clarence. He was so relaxed and snoring. I began my prayer to God, pleading for direction and deliverance for my household. As I turned my body away from Clarence to get comfortable, right there in front of me stood an entity I had never seen before. Its circular head was trimmed in bright white lights and had an empty face with no features. It had neither arms nor legs and its body, which was shaped like a triangle, was filled with thousands of white lights. I held my breath as the entity walked towards me and then fell on me. As I looked up at the ceiling, millions of white lights showered down on me; it was magical. This strange feeling came over me, giving me a peace, I'd never felt before.

I just lay there. After having gone through so much in the past year, I had finally developed that boldness and courage that God could only give me. I knew no one, but He had placed this power on me. He was allowing me to experience these spiritual encounters for a reason. "Why me?" I wondered. I still don't understand any of this right now, but I believe I will one day.

"Life is not a problem to be solved,

but a reality to be experienced."

~Soren Kierkegaard~

~Chapter 20~

Women Answering the Call's Bible study was on fire tonight! As I ministered the word coming from the Book of Job, I shared his trials and struggles and how he had lost many things, including all his children, wealth, health, and high status. You see, Job was a righteous man who stood firm on the word of God, no matter what. The adversary petitioned God to prove Job was not who God said He was. So, God permitted Satan to consume Job, but with one exception: Satan couldn't take Job's life.

While driving home from Bible study, I sincerely thought about what I had just spoken about and how the trials and tribulations affected my life in many areas. No, I wasn't an upright, sinless individual like Job, but I felt like the modern-day 'Jobette.' After Bible study on Thursdays, I was guaranteed the silent treatment for a day or two unless I purchased a bottle of Hennessey to bribe Clarence into being decent towards me.

After grabbing a bottle of water out of the refrigerator and quietly climbing the stairs to not stir Clarence out of his sleep, I was almost too afraid to open the drawer to retrieve my nightgown. Tiptoeing to the bathroom, I quickly scrubbed my body in the shower, dried off, and grabbed the silk headscarf to cover my wrapped hair. Okay, God, so far so good. I prayed for peace and a good night's sleep on my knees. Slipping into the bed and positioning myself next to Clarence, I looked out the corner of my eye towards him, and the song lyrics I'd heard on the radio that morning played in my head: "There's a stranger in my house... It took a while to figure out he wasn't who he had said he was. He has to be someone else... because he wouldn't touch me like that... nor treat me like he does... although I carry his last name... I'm having a problem figuring out exactly who he is."

The Bible says the enemy comes to kill, steal, and destroy. I wondered, could I be sleeping with the enemy? I trusted and believed this stranger. I fell in love with him. I even married him. What does this stranger want from me? Is there anything left for him to take? He stole my heart. He shattered my dreams. And he destroyed our love. I have got to find a way to get away from this stranger who obviously is...the enemy.

"Wanna fly; you got to give up the crap

that weighs you down."

~Toni Morrison~

~Chapter 21~

The phone rang, startling me out of my deep sleep. It was six thirty am, Tuesday, December 23, before Christmas Eve. "Mama, we're only an hour away. Will you please have some grits and salmon croquettes ready?" Vertisa pleaded. Lying there, I thought about everything I needed to do before Christmas Eve, but first on the to-do list was to mop the tiles downstairs where our two Shih Tzus, Jazzy and Butchie resided.

Looking towards heaven, I prayed for peace in my home and a joyful holiday. Though Clarence had repeatedly stated, "It's not going to be a merry Christmas," he'd recently had a complete change of heart regarding all holidays, saying, "There will never be any other holiday, including birthdays, celebrated in our house again." Finally forcing myself out of bed, I speedily brushed my teeth, washed my face, and changed into Capri's and a t-shirt to get things in order. As I briskly swooshed the mop against the family room tile, Clarence walked in, stepping on the wet floor with both dogs, which were also wet—and hyper—from their bath, under his arms. "Clarence, please put them behind the gate in the hallway so they won't trample the floor, I'm trying to clean up their crap." "You don't tell me what to do, Vanady!" he yelled. Oh God, it's too early in the morning. Not today! Clarence grabbed the TV remote off the console, headed for the liquor cabinet, and poured himself a glass of Hennessey for breakfast. Without saying a word, I picked Butchie up first and placed him on the other side of the doggie gate so I could finish mopping. The next thing I knew, Clarence had jumped up off the couch and said, "Don't touch my freaking dogs!"

I explained to him that I would soon finish, and the dogs would be able to wander, but I needed to get the urine and crap off the floor. I then picked Jazzy up to place her on the other side of the gate, but I was met with a forceful push and profane words. Almost falling backwards, I grabbed the counter to balance myself. "Listen, Clarence, now that was a free one! Don't you ever put your hands on me again!"

He snickered and said, "I paid for those darn dogs, and I can do what the hell I want to with them." Then, this fool put the soaking wet dogs on my suede sofa. Okay, he wants to play games this morning. He picked the right day darn, I thought. I'm not in the mood. As he searched the guide channels on the TV, I stood before it and told him I was not moving until he put the dogs on the other side of the gate. I noticed the evil look on his face as he flipped the channels, sipped on his "breakfast," and hummed out loud. He became irritated as I started to hum, too, and leaned from side to side, blocking his view. "Move, Vanady," he said. "No, I'm not budging, Clarence. Why are you being so nasty this early in the morning?" "Oh, well, I guess I will watch TV upstairs since you won't move." "Do what you want to do, sir, just leave me the hell alone."

As I progressed in my mopping, it suddenly hit me: Oh, my goodness, he will take my car keys. Running upstairs, I was startled when I pushed open the double doors to the main suite and saw that the lunatic had placed both wet dogs on my side of our bed atop my cream-colored comforter. He had made it clear he would ruin the holiday season for everyone and was off to a pretty good start.

Grabbing the dogs and placing them on the floor, Clarence leaped off the bed and charged at me, pushing me against the bedpost. Victor heard the mayhem in the room a few doors down and ran into the room. As I tried to grab my car keys from Clarence's grip, he dug his nails deep down into my hand, literally drawing blood. As we tussled with one another, my son yelled out, "Get off my mama!" Clarence's expression was very dark and evil; he was in a zone. My son grabbed Clarence off of me, and their fight began. The fight went from the bedroom to the bathroom, with me trying everything I could to separate them. I realized he was trying to kill my son; he was so strong. As he continuously stabbed my son in the head with the car keys, I noticed the blood gushing from my son's head. "Clarence, stop!" I screamed, but he didn't hear me; he was on another planet. Oh Lord, this man is going to kill my child. Please tell me what to do! It's as if he's the Incredible Hulk! He is just too strong! I had never seen anything like this in my life, and it was happening right before my eyes. All I knew was that I had to get this demon off my son. I grabbed the plastic broom and threatened Clarence that I would use it. As the struggle continued in the bathroom, my son was giving Clarence a run for his money, jamming his head into the towel rack, and drawing blood. It was something out of a movie scene. I frantically ran for the phone, threatening Clarence that I would call 911.

As time stood still for a moment, he spun his head around, just like in The Exorcist, looked me dead in my eyes, and let out this loud, screeching, demonic laugh, stating, "I'm going to be a bad boy!"

"Many and most moments go by with us hardly aware of their passage. But love, hate, and fear cause time to snag you, to drag you down like a spider's web holding fast to a doomed fly's wings."

~Walter Mosley~

~Chapter 22~

"This is 911. May I help you?" asked the dispatcher. "Please, we need help; my husband is acting erratically and physically attacking me and my son. It's like he's possessed with something." "Are you still at home, ma'am?" "Yes, we are." "I need you to grab your son and go outside the house immediately. I have dispatched units to your home." Victor and I ran downstairs and outside, standing under the shaded palm tree and waiting for help. Finally, seven minutes later, the police officers showed up. Though we were outside, I could see that Clarence was now sitting in the living room area with a washcloth, dabbing his head because the front double doors were open. As he caught a glimpse of me staring at him, he smiled.

The officers separated Victor and me, drilling us about the domestic altercation. I found it weird that although I'd made the call, the officers gave Clarence more attention than Victor and me. Question after question, something didn't feel right. As I looked at the skinny Caucasian male officer, there was something about him that seemed eerie; he wasn't like the friendly police officers who'd taken me to jail when I was three years old.

Just as my daughters drove up in front of the house, the female officer told me to turn around and put my hands behind my back. "What!" I yelled. She began to read me my rights as the other officer pushed my son toward the patrol car. Victor was screaming, "I did it! She had nothing to do with it! Let her go."

I yelled at the officer, "I'm a mother! I'm a business owner! I'm a woman of God! What are you doing?" She told me to calm down, and I got louder, yelling, "What are you doing? I called you! He hurt my son, and he hurt me!"

"Ma'am, please calm down," the female officer said. My daughters jumped out of the car, running towards me as I was shoved into the patrol car. "Oh my God, what's happening?" I asked. My heart was beating so fast, and I was hyperventilating. I was also sweating profusely, frantic, emotional, and I was scared.

While they took me to be booked, Victor was put into a separate car and escorted to the hospital for his bruises and then to the juvenile detention center. The bottom line is that I was on my way to facing the most significant life challenge.

As we pulled up to the Pembroke Pines Precinct, I was crying, and I tried to explain what had happened to the driver of the police car. He was kind and stated, "They will straighten everything out." He tried to console me through his words. However, as I was led into the station and then booked, my nerves were out of control. A person living with claustrophobia, when they closed the cell door, I literally couldn't breathe. Okay, God, I can do this I told myself. I am innocent. I know you are with me, and I trust you.

Sitting alone in that cell, I tried to be brave, I tried to be strong, but those demons showed up and kept reminding me of my fears about closed-in places. I jumped off the iron bench, banged on the door, and yelled, "I can't breathe!" The wrinkled, mean-spirited, silver-haired lady told me to shut up and sit down; I obliged. Praying like never before, I asked God for strength and courage.

As time passed, I felt jittery and cold. I had no one to talk to, and I felt that tight strain in my private area. I needed to pee so badly! Before I got off the bench, I prayed aloud, "God, I don't know what you're doing, but again, I trust you, I need thee." Banging on the steel cell door again, I asked to speak to the supervisor. "Sir, I promise you," I pleaded. "If you can just crack the door, I can do this. I can't breathe, sir," I stated. He looked at me, turned to the male officer, and said, "It's the holiday, leave the door open for her." "Thank you, God! I know that you're with me," I whispered. Within an hour, they came to transfer me from the Pembroke Pines Precinct to the Davie Precinct. Here we go again. Okay God, you have shown me mercy, but I need you to see me through this journey, whatever it is.

As they reviewed my information at the new precinct, I thought, remember Philippians 4:13. You can do all things through Christ who strengthens you. Hold on to that, girl. Looking at the clock, time was frozen, and so was I. As I shivered in the cold cell, I prayed for favor. You did it before, and I know you can do it again. Please open the door like you did at the Pembroke Pines Precinct.

I knocked on the door, and an elderly gentleman approached me and asked, "May I help you?" Being as honest as possible, I told him about my claustrophobia and that I would sit still if he would crack open the steel door. He looked at me with this angelic countenance and told the lady sitting behind the desk to keep the door open and give me whatever I needed. Okay, God, I thought, You are up to something. What assignment have you placed in my lap?

After being awakened from a quick nap, I was told, "You are being extradited to the Broward County facility." As I was led out of the precinct, the elderly officer gave a caring wink and nod. The only woman amongst several men, they opened the steel police vehicle with no windows and led the male prisoners into the vehicle. As they closed the door, I thought, I guess I'll sit up front with the driver. Leading me toward the front of the vehicle, the gentleman stopped and opened the door to a steel cabin with a bench but no window. "I'm not getting in there!" I yelled. "You have to, ma'am," the officer said. "We cannot put you in the back with the men; you must be separated, lady." "There is neither legroom nor windows," I said. "Listen, ma'am, you can do this," the chubby, friendly officer stated.

Realizing I had no choice, I extended my left leg and pulled my body into the steel cab. Hearing the sound of the engine roar, I felt like the metal was closing in on me. I was losing it. With only a bird's eye view through the peephole to the driver, I banged on the steel walls, screaming, "I can't breathe! Let me out!" The officer jumped out of the driver's seat, opened the door, and said, "Now, ma'am, I need you to trust me. If I take you out, you will have to go inside, and they will have to evaluate you, and there's much paperwork involved. You told me earlier that you wanted to get home for Christmas. You won't, ma'am, because it will take about fourteen hours before the psychologist decides, and you will miss Christmas." "But, sir," I cried, "I can't breathe." "Listen, ma'am. This is what I want you to do. I want you to put your eyes directly on that hole and not look to your left or right, just keep your eyes on the road and I promise I will get you down to Broward as fast as I can." I had no other choice. I had to find the courage and the strength to do this. As the engine roared, so did the fire in my soul. I began to recite the Lord's Prayer out loud, over and over again. I needed to get to my children. I needed to get home for Christmas. I needed God to see me through.

"You really can change the world if you care enough."

~Marian Wright Edelman~

~Chapter 23~

"Turn to your left! Now your right! Look at me, ma'am, and say, 'Criminal!'" They were being sarcastic and acting like total idiots. "We need her taken upstairs, changed, and put in block C2 with the felons."

I did everything they told me to do. Slowly, I realized that the situation was more significant than me; it was a spiritual assignment. Changing into the wrinkled beige smelly jumpsuit, I felt jittery all over again. Okay, Vanady, get yourself together, girl, I encouraged myself.

The inmates of Cellblock C2 included murderers, thieves, drug traffickers, child molesters, and the like. I saw a mix of women of different ethnicities, ages, and backgrounds as I looked around. A few were crying, a handful played cards on the iron picnic-type tables, at least four of them were gathered in a corner talking, and the others were spread out sitting on the floor or benches, minding their own business. Mumbling to myself, I asked God to order my steps and not allow this experience to be in vain.

God led me to the iron red picnic-type table with iron benches. As one of the inmates at the table stared at me, I thought, I've heard many stories about what women do to other women in jail, but Vanady isn't going down like that. Remember, Roe is known for the ability to fight physically and spiritually.

"Hi ma'am, my name is Samaria. What is your name?" the dark haired masculine young lady said to me. "Hi, Samaria, my name is Vanady." "What brings you here, Ms. Vanady?" she asked.

Well, my husband lied and said I physically assaulted him, so I'm in for domestic violence. And you? "I stabbed my Aunt Claire eighteen times, and she died," she nonchalantly said. "Wow, why would you do something like that to your family member?" It's a long story that goes back to my childhood… Anyways, she had it coming." Tell me a little about yourself and where you come from, Sam, if you don't mind me calling you that. Oh, it's okay, everyone calls me that or Sammy because they say I have male features. "I don't think so, Sam," I blurted out. "I like your nice, short hairstyle; your eyes are beautiful, girl." Really!" she said to me.

Samaria, have you looked in the mirror lately? I do sometimes, but not really. You see when my mother died, I was only four; my aunt raised my brother and me. She kissed the ground my little brother walked on, but she always reminded me that she didn't want to take me in and that I was a cursed ugly duckling like my Father. "Well, your aunt is gone and can't defend herself. All I know is you are very pretty and seem to be a nice person. I am nice, Vanady, but most people don't understand me. They say I'm bipolar or schizophrenic. But I'm really creative and lively and can change my mind about anything anytime I feel like it. You are right, Sam. It's your life, and you get to live it how you want. The only person you have to please is the Father. I never knew my father. No, Sam, I'm talking about your Heavenly Father, God. I don't think God likes me very much, she said woefully. Why would you say something so untrue about God? Well, He took everything away from me, starting with my mother. He allowed my aunt to abuse me and treat me like garbage, and when I went to school, the kids called me 'smelly, dirty, ugly, and crazy. The boys never asked me out for dates. I didn't have a good upbringing.

Well, Sam, you may not understand what I am about to say, but all those people who wronged or hurt you didn't know the wonderfully made Samaria sitting next to me. Sometimes, people can be cruel, but you must know who you are and believe God doesn't make any mistakes. God cares about you. How do you know He does, Ms. Vanady? Because He sent me here to tell you that today, I responded. May I sit next to you, and maybe you can tell me more about God? Of course, Sam!"

She sat beside me and said, "I don't know much about God except what my aunt would say sometimes. She didn't understand Him either, but when problems came, she would yell out, "God help me!' Well, Sam, I don't know how long I will be here, but I will share everything I know about Him with you. Okay, it's not like we can go anywhere anyway… Go for it, she openly said. Let us pray first, I insisted. Pray for what? she innocently asked. Sam, I always consult with God before I do anything. Okay, whatever makes you happy Ms. Vanady."

As the Holy Spirit guided my mouth and words, I didn't realize how loud I had become. All I knew was that the anointing was all over me, and I was on fire! Upon finishing the prayer, when I opened my eyes, several ladies stood around me. Please, lady, an elderly woman with missing teeth said, will you pray for me too? Then the young, nervous Hispanic girl biting her fingernails asked, can I be next after her? Then, the toothpick-thin African American woman with dirty fingernails asked me to pray for her, too.

Oh God, they are coming from everywhere, asking for prayer. This time of year is sentimental because it's the holiday season. One after the other, just about the whole cell block wants little ole Roe to pray for them. Please guide me, Father. I want to help every one of them. I want to make a difference in their lives by sharing You. I don't want to get in trouble with the correctional officers, though, so cover me in the blood, I pleaded.

God then led me to have the women sit in a circle. I stood in the middle, sharing who I was and why I was there. Then, the Holy Spirit led me to sing a song. Sing what, God? I asked. "Sing 'Yes, Jesus Loves Me,'" The Holy Spirit whispered. I opened my mouth, and the words flowed out like Niagara Falls. "Yes, Jesus loves me! Yes, Jesus loves me. Yes, Jesus loves me, for the bible tells me so!" In the next stanza, the ladies joined in, singing as if they were still those little girls in church, feeling that song. It was beautiful.

When the singing stopped, my body stood there, but God took it from there. I remember that by the time I finished sharing God, tears flowed; everyone was hugging one another, trying to touch me, and wanting to know more. Even a couple of correctional officers looked on, pleased. God had shown up and showed out! We had church right there in Cellblock C2.

"Try to be a rainbow in someone's cloud."

~Maya Angelou~

~Chapter 24~

"Lights out, ladies!" the male correctional officer announced after I was stuffed into a cell the size of a tiny walk-in closet. There were at least six of us assigned to the first cell on the bottom floor. As the screeching steel electric door closed and locked us in for the night, I had to be brave and not give in to the jittery, nervous feeling. I had an assignment that needed to be fulfilled. We sat on the concrete floor, some of us with mats and some without, and I knew it would be an interesting night. As I looked at each of their faces, I wondered who would break first. Within minutes, the older African American mother whose sixteen-year-old daughter had attacked her, causing her, in turn, to whip her daughter, broke down. As I held her in my arms, I could feel the beat of her racing heart. Mama, you must calm down, or you're going to have a heart attack," I whispered into her ear. But you don't understand, Ms. Vanady, I was only protecting myself and would never physically abuse anyone. I love my daughter; it's just that she has become so disrespectful lately. She sneaks out of the house at night; her school calls me at least twice a week because she's skipping class. She talks back to me and tells me what she will or will not do. I just couldn't take her disrespect anymore, so I slapped her and hit her on the arm with my hairbrush. You see, my daughter is fair-skinned, and the few licks on her arms showed red bruises. Why would she call the police? How could she do something like this to me? I'm her mother? I can't breathe. I got to get out of here!

Listen, Mama, I know what you are feeling. This is new territory for me too. We're going to be alright. Trust me.

One by one, God used me to comfort them as they faced their own personal demons in that cell. Once I got the last one to sleep, I needed to release my bowels so badly. As I looked at the feces-crusted steel stool that reeked of urine, I could barely catch my breath from its stench. My stomach was boiling like a pot on top of a stove, and Lord knows I didn't need to add to the reeking stench. And to top it all off, there was no tissue to wipe anyway. God, please let me hold it in until tomorrow morning, I whimpered. Squeezing my buttocks and legs tightly together, I held it in as I lay stretched on the thin mat that seemed more suited for a toddler. It was so cold, and the thin, smelly wool blanket was doing me no justice. I felt it coming on; the claustrophobia spirit had been awakened.

Encouraging myself, I whispered, Vanady, you just talked to these women about the spirit of fear and everything else. You've got to lead by example. Get it together, girl. Closing my eyes, I prayed to my Heavenly Father for the courage and wisdom to face the long night that was ahead of me. As the tears rolled down my face, I thought of how I had endured so much for one man. I thought of how I'd only wanted to make my marriage work and help save someone who simply didn't want to be saved. I remembered Hannah from the Bible as my mouth mumbled words from my heart to God. As I ended my prayer, I opened my eyes and witnessed something that could have only come out of a movie scene. As the white dancing lights in the ceiling circled and then showered down on me, I was in awe. Then this calm voice said, "Vanady, you're going home tomorrow." The voice instructed me to grab the thin mat from one of the ladies who had gone home earlier and to cover my body with it. I obeyed the voice and laid back down. The next thing I knew, they were waking us up for breakfast. I'd slept the entire night without any interruptions. Wow, my God is so faithful!

Later, while sitting at the iron table, the ladies were so kind, telling me they would look out for me and that there was a forty-eight-hour mandatory cooling off period for domestic violence. "Oh no, but thank you, ladies," I said. "I'm going home today!" They chuckled and said, "Girl, do you understand what the word mandatory means? You will not be going home today, Ms. Vanady, but we got your back."

I shared with them my spiritual encounter from the night before and told them that the voice had said I was going home and that I believed it. Where do you come from, lady? they asked sarcastically. You are not only crazy; you are delusional! Boldly, I stood up and said out loud so everyone could hear me, "Listen! Yesterday I told you about my Heavenly Father who loves me and each one of you! I told you He cannot lie, and His word does not come back void! I told you that He will never leave nor forsake you and that He will even carry you when you can't carry yourself! I told you about His amazing grace and mercy! But most important, I told you He would have the final say-so! Now, if I don't go home today, everything I told you about Him was a lie! But remember, He cannot lie! So, if I do not go home today, you can go back to your old idols or other gods, and everything I said was bull-crap! But if I do go home, you will see His Power and how He is the final Judge!"

They started talking quietly amongst themselves, some even giggling, but I didn't care, God had spoken. However, I did find a corner and reminded

God of His word from the night before and that everything regarding these women spirituality was in jeopardy. "God, you must set me free today, I whimpered. Everything about You and me is on the line here. I know you will deliver." These were my final words to God before the officer came in with the list of names for the arraignment.

I stood tall and unmovable as they called out name after name, not blinking an eye. When he announced, "This is the last name, and everyone else needs to return to their cell," for a few seconds, my heart stopped. Out of nowhere, just before he shouted the final name, a cool wind overtook me and Vanady Alexander had made the cut. Everyone looked at each other in disbelief.

With a smile, I turned and meaningfully said, "I told you I was going home today. I told you God can't lie and He has the final say-so." Some of their mouths were wide open as one of them said, "Well, you still got to go before the judge." I said to her, I have already faced the Judge of judges, and He has set me free!"

"Well, we will see," the slick-mouthed redhead said as they lined us up. Of course, I was last because my name was at the bottom of the list.

Suited-up in beige, Vanady Alexander and the selected ladies of cellblock C2 walked in unison through the hollow hallways to face "their judge."

"My life is my message."

~Mahatma Gandhi~

~Chapter 25~

Being the last woman inmate would work out to my advantage as they sat us against the wall on the hard splintered benches. My, my, my, what the hell is this? I looked around the room, taking note of the big video screen and male inmates on the other side of the room. It was not what I'd pictured when I'd watched Judge Judy or Perry Mason on television. The male Caucasian public defender stopped at each inmate, asking them if anyone was low-income and needed his services. When he got to me, I asked him the criteria for representation for my case, and of course, once I shared my salary, I wasn't qualified.

Sitting at the very end of the bench, I was within arm's reach of the deputy behind the computer. "Sir," I said as politely as possible. "Will you please check my name to see if I qualify for bail?" No problem, he said. As I gave him my information, he began typing, and then he looked at me gloomily and said, "I'm sorry, Ms. Alexander. You have no bail."

For some reason, I didn't panic. I just bowed my head and prayed from my heart. Amazingly, a voice whispered, "Vanady, call the public defender back over and ask him if he could represent you just for today." What? I thought to myself. The man told me I didn't qualify because of my income; I would look like a fool. But being Vanady, I obeyed the voice. I raised and waved my hand at the public defender. He looked at me awkwardly and then slowly stood and made his way over to me.

"Yes, may I help you?" he asked. Sir, I was wondering if, just for today, can you please, represent me? He reached into his navy jacket, took out a silver-plated ink pen and a small notepad, and asked me my name. As I gave it to him, my voice was shaking. I was shaking. He turned and walked away without asking me a single question.

The judge, who turned out to be a magistrate, was in another room filled with family members and other concerned individuals. Case after case, the magistrate had no mercy. He slammed the book at everyone, and the public defender never moved to represent anybody. I thought this silver-haired old Caucasian man was the Grinch who stole Christmas. What the hell is this? For simple misdemeanors, bails were set unrealistically high. Lord, I've been charged with a felony for attempted murder; I can only imagine.

"Stop, Vanady!" The voice screamed in my head. God, I'm losing it; help me, please! Okay, calm down, Roe, I encouraged myself. Remembering how fearless Roe was, I needed her to replace Vanady! Sitting straight up and raising my head high, I slowly rested my back against the wall, twiddled my thumbs, and waited for my turn. It broke my heart to witness the tears and cries of the women who weren't going to make it home for Christmas tomorrow to be with their children. However, I knew I had to trust God like never before.

"Ms. Vanady Alexander, please approach the podium!" the officer shouted. Something had happened; I wasn't shaking anymore and walked with authority as a woman warrior. All the eyes of the women of Cellblock C2 were fixed on me. I had to "Stand Tall," despite what it looked like or what the outcome would be.

"Ms. Alexander," the judge said clearly. "I see you are a resident of Broward County. How many years, ma'am?" I have lived in this county for thirteen years, sir. "I see you're highly educated, Ms. Alexander, what happened? Why would you assault your spouse with a deadly weapon, ma'am? Do you know you could have killed him?" Sir, things didn't happen the way he said they did. He lied about me, I replied.

Next thing I knew, my sister Judith, who was in the other room, asked to be heard by the judge. Oh, my goodness, I thought, my family has packed the courtroom. However, I could only see them through the video screen. My sister shared her position as a United States Officer with the judge and told him she would put her credibility on the line, earnestly stating, "My sister Vanady would never do something like this." The judge said, "Okay, sit down, ma'am. I've heard enough."

My heart sank as I looked at the faces of the ladies who were expecting a miracle on my behalf. It was like they needed to believe in something. They needed God to do what I'd said He would do. They needed hope. In the blink of an eye, the silent public defender stood. I could feel the blood pumping in my heart, and it was racing. "Your Honor," he said, "look at that police report, sir, It just doesn't add up."

The silver-haired magistrate picked up the report, leaned back in his chair, and glanced at the paper. You could have heard a pin drop; that room had dead silence. The judge picked up his gavel and hit it on the solid wood, announcing, "Vanady Alexander, I set bail at $1000.00." The courtroom erupted in celebration from the ladies of cellblock C2. The judge hit the gavel, shouting, "Order in the court, ladies!"

"God, you did it!" I shouted. "We did it! You mean to tell me all I need is $100.00, and I can go home?" The voice whispered, "I'm proud of you, daughter." I replied, "Thank you, Father."

When I returned to cellblock C2, I discovered that word had already gotten upstairs before me and that the rest of the inmates knew. They hugged me, jumped up and down, and thanked me for sharing God with them. I was so happy and honored, yet saddened at the same time as I watched the tears flow from those not as fortunate as me. I asked them to come into the circle once more before I left. As I lay hands on each one of them individually, I pleaded the blood of Jesus over their lives. I prayed for God to lead them on the path of righteousness and give them wisdom in their day-to-day doings. I prayed for their situations and asked God to extend His mercy and grace. Lastly, I asked God to save their souls and deliver them. It was finished. I was finished.

The correctional officer beckoned for me to come over to the desk. He said, "Ms. Alexander, you are scheduled to go home around seven pm because you're last on the list. However, you remind me of my mother. She was a praying woman, too. I'm moving you from the bottom to the top. Now go say your goodbyes. They will be coming for you shortly."

After changing into my Capris and t-shirt, I walked on air and strode down the corridor. Despite my overnight stay and challenging ride to Broward County Correctional Facility, I still looked good. Someone shouted, "Let's get her autograph! That's Whitney Houston!" I looked at my two daughters, smiled, and sipped the outside air as if taking my first breath of life. Thank you, Lord. As you said, I will make it home in time for Christmas!

"In the end, it's not the years

in your life that count.

It's the life in your years."

~Abraham Lincoln~

~Chapter 26~

How was I supposed to go forth with my life? I was stuck in neutral. Even after filing for a restraining order and for divorce two days after being released from jail, in time for the Christmas holiday, as crazy as it might sound, I wondered if I'd made the right decision. I have such a heart for people. Forgiveness was instilled in me at a very young age. No matter how my times my siblings and I had argued and fought, my parents would not allow us to go to sleep without making up. Why can't I be like most people? Vindictive, revengeful, cold-hearted, and call my male family members to kick his butt? God knows I did what I had to do for my mental, emotional, physical, spiritual, and psychological state, or Clarence Alexander would have killed me one way or the other. I asked God, why didn't my prayers and fasting work? God, I told you I would give it all up if you would just save my husband and my marriage. After all the pain, sleepless nights, fighting off demonic forces, HIGH spiritual warfare, tears, prayers, and turning the other cheek, you mean to tell me it boils down to this?

The month was February and it had been two months since I'd last seen Clarence. I wonder, does he have any remorse or even care about what happened to the kids and me? I needed to stay strong, but this was the biggest financial, emotional, spiritual roller-coaster of a challenge of my life. My Mercedes-Benz was two months past due. The electricity had been cut off for a couple of days and the Direct TV cable satellite account had been closed. My salary could barely cover the house note, water, gas, and car insurance. I had maxed out all my credit cards on legal fees and incidentals for my small publishing company. I was not financially prepared for this enormous test. I was drowning and in need of a life jacket.

As the months went by and the bills stacked higher, I was living totally off of faith. I prayed so hard and so long that sometimes I would wake up the next morning asleep on the floor. What did I or my ancestors do to make me deserve all this pain? That summer was the roughest I ever lived through. I will never forget how miserably hot that August Sunday afternoon was. The air conditioning had gone out the day before. If Hell felt anything like this, I certainly didn't want any part of it!

Vanessa quietly came down the stairs holding her stomach, and said, Mama, I'm so hungry. Opening the refrigerator and freezer doors, I stared at the half-filled pitcher of water and single stick of butter and sighed. "Okay, Vanessa, what would you like to eat today, sweetheart?" I asked.

"Ummm, I want some good ole fried chicken!" "Okay, baby. I need to go upstairs and check on something first before we go out." "Okay, Mama," she replied. God, I had three closets full of clothing and a brand-new Mercedes-Benz outside, and I was living in an upscale gated community, but I didn't have one dollar to my name. I had pawned my wedding rings and anything else of value to help cover household expenses. What could I do? My child and I were famished, and to top it all off, we were sweating like pigs. In your word, God, I prayed, You said that You would supply ALL my needs according to Your riches in Heaven. I'm here on earth, passing through, but right now Lord, we need an earthly blessing. We are hungry!

Closing my bedroom door and pressing my way to my closet on bended knee, I went to work reminding God of His promises and petitioning Him for help. Out of nowhere, I heard the Holy Spirit speak, "Daughter check your purses, slacks, and the drawers." I yelled out to Vanessa to come upstairs. "Baby, I need you to go through all the drawers downstairs and look for coins, okay, sweetie?" Okay, Mama," she replied. It was like we were on a scavenger hunt looking for lost treasure. Every time Vanessa or I found a coin, we would yell out to each other how much. Searching through my Coach, Gucci, and Louis Vuitton purses, I found plenty of coins. "Mama, I found a quarter and a dime in the corner of the drawer next to the stove!" "Great, baby! We are looking for treasure, so you got to listen closely at what we are going to do next, okay?" "Okay, Mama," she replied. "I will take the family room, and you take the living room. We're going to go down the sides of the sofas and loveseats with our hands and dig for coins." "Yes! Buried treasure! Vanessa exclaimed. At the end of the scavenger hunt, Vanessa and I had collected a total of nine dollars and fifty-five cents. She was so excited! I heard you, Father, I prayed in thanks. You lead, and I will follow.

Grabbing the car keys, Vanessa and I headed out the door. Once we were in the car, I saw that the gas tank was empty. Oh no! How am I going to get to work tomorrow? I needed to put at least five dollars in the gas tank, which would leave me with only four dollars and fifty-five cents for food.

Once inside Publix, I priced the chicken, flour, and cooking oil. I didn't have enough coins to even purchase the six-pack of chicken wings. God, help us, I pleaded. Leaving the store empty-handed, I drove into the nearby Shell gas station and pumped $5.00 into the tank. Okay, Ms. Cortez owes me

$20.00 and said she would repay me tomorrow. That would at least see Vanessa and I through the week.

Placing the nozzle back onto the pump, I looked up to heaven and prayed for a sign that everything was going to be all right. Going around the rear of the car to get in, the red and white marquee with the white-haired man with a mustache caught my attention. The words on the sign read, "Three-piece dark chicken special with two sides, $3.99." After exhaling and letting out a loud "Thank you, Lord," I told Vanessa how good God is and that things would get better for us. Placing the four dollars and fifty-five cents into my anxious daughter's hands to buy the meal was like giving her my last breath. Vanessa quickly opened the door and skipped inside the Kentucky Fried Chicken restaurant to purchase our supper. Sitting and awaiting her return, the tears rolled down my face as I poured my heart out in prayer, thanking God for making a way out of no way. I looked up, and even though it was a sunny, clear Sunday in Pembroke Pines, Florida, there in the sky were two of the most beautiful rainbows one could ever see. Reaching into my purse, I pulled out my notebook and pen and began writing:

Looking through my purse
searching all the drawers
Checking pants pockets
hoping to find a few dollars

It's dinner time
there is no rice or meat
This is getting hard
we can barely eat

No money in the bank

nor a cent on credit too

Father, I need a blessing

tell me what to do?

The enemy is at work

trying to break me down

But I am holding on

I know You're still around

You have never forsaken me

I know this is just a test

I will continue to STAND

and give You my best

This…

Too…

Shall…

Pass,

I will make it through!

Then I will be elevated

and receive the promises too

To God be the Glory!

And yes, that was the BEST darn FRIED CHICKEN I ever tasted!!!

"Freedom is never given; it is won."

~A. Philip Randolph~

~Chapter 27~

This day had been a long time coming. As I look over the selected jurors, I pondered, Do they really understand their duty here today? Do they know that my freedom, career, even lifestyle is in their hands? Do they realize that the outcome of this case could very well impact the rest of my life? You know, life is funny; no one ever thinks they might go through something like this. As the judge beckoned for the prosecutor to bring in the state's key witness, my entire body went numb all over. You see, I hadn't seen Clarence since the domestic dispute ten months ago. I wonder if he's changed. I asked myself. Has my estranged ex-husband finally gotten it right with God? I really hope he does the right thing today, I whimpered. As he raised his right hand to tell the truth and nothing but the truth and place his left hand on the bible, I knew he was still in bondage, serving Satan. Question after question, lie after lie, I couldn't believe what I was hearing. This idiot wanted my freedom! He wanted to destroy me!

Again, I asked God, Could he be who he says he is? Is he really Satan's son? I was in awe at what was coming out of his mouth. I literally felt embarrassed for him. His sweet mother would have been ashamed to know she'd given birth to this deceitful, manipulative, evil, liar of a son. God, how could I have been so blind and foolish? How could I have not seen through his smoke screen? Was I that vulnerable and weak to have let someone slip in under the radar like this? I tell you; this was scary!

As Clarence rose and walked away from the witness chair, our eyes locked for the first time. Glancing at each other, just our looks would have cut any cement brick in half. Love had definitely been replaced by something else. Tomorrow, though, my son and I would get our chance to share the real truth.

Returning home that evening, I decided that if I was going to believe God for what He said He would do, I could not worry. I ordered a pepperoni pizza, along with some wings with celery, carrots, and bleu cheese for Victor, Vanessa, and me. After a warm shower, the Holy Spirit led me to my bible reading for the night, Psalms 91. Verse 15 captivated my spirit: "He will call on me, and I will answer him; I will be with him in trouble, I will deliver him and honor him. With long life I will satisfy him and show my salvation." Wow! Father, would you do all of that for a sinner like me?

Falling to my knees, the tears welled up in my eyes. Despite my disobedience, self-righteous ways, sins, shortcomings, and wrong choices, my grandmama's words from years ago had finally come to life. Astonished, I asked, you mean to tell me that God still loved me despite my mistakes? Grandmama was absolutely right; God loves me. After praying, I fell into one of the best nights of rest I have ever had in my entire life. However, the next morning, as I got up off my knees, I thought of the last ten months of my life. I thought of the domestic altercation itself. I thought of the overnight stay in jail. I thought of the emotional and physical pain that had been afflicted on my son and me. I thought of the thousands of dollars in legal fees I had incurred. I thought of the many days I'd had to leave my job because of depositions, court hearings, and attorney's office visits. I thought of my very life! The emotion of anger tried to rise up, but as I cried out to God, He touched me and removed that feeling.

The drive to the Broward County courthouse via I-95 with Victor the next morning went surprisingly smoothly. Even as I drove up to find parking, there it was, a space waiting just for me, the perfect parking spot with a coined meter. Only God knew what a blessing this was; all the legal fees had me scraping for every cent I could get my hand on. God, maybe this is a sign!

My key witness was Victor. Now in his first year of college, I'd had to fly him home for today's court case. I needed him to share with the jurors and judge what really happened that morning. My son was awesome, he simply told the truth. Then it was my turn on the witness stand. I spoke with clarity and honesty. My mouth was just the instrument because the Holy Spirit had taken over.

As I stood in front of the judge, jurors, attorneys, clerks, and other attendees of the courtroom, I recounted the hellish experiences that my children and I had endured. Their faces showed astonishment and sympathy as I spoke. After I stepped down from the witness stand, I felt weak in my knees. However, the Holy Spirit touched me once again, giving me the strength, I needed to return to my seat. At three thirty p.m., the judge dismissed the jurors to the restroom and announced where they needed to go and what they needed to do. While the judge was away, I lifted my head up and took deep breaths to calm myself. Suddenly, the jurors and judge returned to the courtroom, and the big clock on the wall read three thirty-four p.m. In just four minutes, those wonderful jurors gave me back my life by giving their verdict. I am so grateful to God for being there for me. He saved me and delivered me, just as He promised. He listened to my prayers and answered them. God blessed me for fasting and staying committed to Him. He kept my mind safe when I was on the verge of losing it. He was there throughout the night when I was walking the floors. He is my true friend who loves me unconditionally. I have overcome my struggles and am now free. Finally, I have found peace.

DEEPEST THOUGHTS

1. Did you know what Spiritual Warfare was prior to reading this book? If yes, what were the red flags for you?

2. Which chapter stood out amongst the others and why?

3. Why do you think Vanady although there were negative behaviors from Clarence, said yes to marriage?

4. What are some lessons you learned from Peace from the Past and how will you apply them to your life?

5. Name three people you want to share this book with:

    1.

    2.

    3.

    Please consider using Peace from the Past as a conversation starter amongst your book clubs, bible study groups, workshops, retreats, conferences, etc. I would appreciate it if you could help me inform more people about the goodness of God by writing a review on Google or Amazon.

    Thank you for choosing to spend your time reading my memoir.

Contact Information

"Peace from the Past"

If you would like to share how this book has helped or encouraged you or to schedule seminars, conferences, speaking engagements, or workshops, please contact:

vgoldenallen@gmail.com

or

info@vjpublishinghouse@gmail.com

PUBLISHING HOUSE, LLC.

"Where Your Stories Are Built, On a Solid Foundation"

www.vjpublishinghouse.com

www.ingramcontent.com/pod-product-compliance
Lightning Source LLC
Chambersburg PA
CBHW072012090426

42740CB00011B/2164